PENGUIN BOOKS

LETTERS HOME

Fergal Keane OBE is one of the BBC's most distinguished correspondents, having worked for the corporation in Northern Ireland, South Africa, Asia and the Balkans. He has been awarded a BAFTA and has been named reporter of the year on television and radio, winning honours from the Royal Television Society and the Sony Radio Awards. He has also been named Reporter of the Year in the Amnesty International Press Awards and won the James Cameron Prize and the Edward R. Murrow Award from the US Overseas Press Association. His other books include *The Bondage of Fear* (Penguin, 1995), *Season of Blood* (Penguin, 1996), winner of the 1995 Orwell Prize, and *Letter to Daniel* (Penguin/BBC, 1996). His new book, *A Stranger's Eye*, is forthcoming from Viking. Fergal Keane was born in London and educated in Ireland, where he keeps a small cottage on the south-east coast.

LETTERS HOME

Fergal Keane

EDITED BY
Tony Grant

PENGUIN BOOKS

PENGUIN BOOKS

Published by the Penguin Group
Penguin Books Ltd, 27 Wrights Lane, London W8 5TZ, England
Penguin Putnam Inc., 375 Hudson Street, New York, New York 10014, USA
Penguin Books Australia Ltd, Ringwood, Victoria, Australia
Penguin Books Canada Ltd, 10 Alcorn Avenue, Toronto, Ontario, Canada M4V 3B2
Penguin Books (NZ) Ltd, Private Bag 102902, NSMC, Auckland, New Zealand

Penguin Books Ltd, Registered Offices: Harmondsworth, Middlesex, England

First published 1999
3 5 7 9 10 8 6 4 2

The acknowledgements on p. ix constitute an extension of this copyright page

Set in 10.5/13.5pt Monotype Joanna
Typeset by Rowland Phototypesetting Ltd, Bury St Edmunds, Suffolk
Printed in England by Clays Ltd, St Ives plc

'A person is a person because of other people'

(SOUTH AFRICAN PROVERB)

CONTENTS

Acknowledgements   ix
Introduction   xi

Part One: From Close to Home

The Fur Trapper   3
In the Heart of the Country   12
Rock 'n' Roll Days   21
The Bass Fishers   27
The Wise Teacher   31
On Spring Street   35
Bullies   39
By Newport Station We Sat Down and Waited   43
What We Talk About When We Talk About
   Carver   47
Leaving Home   52

Part Two: From a European War

The Grave   59
Macedonian Spring   64
'Easy' and the Boys   68
Kukes Nights   72
The Judging of Milosevic   76
Culture Shock in Chiantishire   80
War's End   83

Part Three: From Ireland

Where We Came From   89
Glad, So Glad to be Wrong   96

CONTENTS

The Killing of the Quinns   99
The Day of the Butchers   103
Saving Private Daly   107
The Boys of Summer   111

Part Four: From a Drifting Continent

Au Revoir, Mes Enfants   119
Return to South Africa   136
Cynthia's Story   139
Christmas in Cape Town   144
A Boy Called 'Grenade'   148
Horror in the Mangroves   151
An African Renaissance   154
Seat of the Pants   159

Part Five: From Elsewhere

Farewell to Hong Kong   165
Live and Let Dai   168
Wish You Were Here   172
A Tale of Two Dentists   176
Agony on the Pilgrim Trail   179
A Raw Horse in the Mountains   182
The Impossible Choice   185
Spoiled Idealism   190
The Rape of Michael Blucker   194
The Night Pinochet Got My Neighbours Drunk   197

Index   201

ACKNOWLEDGEMENTS

The author and publishers wish to thank the following who first published or broadcast material that is included here (a number of pieces have been substantially revised):

The Independent for 'Macedonian Spring', '"Easy" and the Boys', 'Kukes Nights', 'The Judging of Milosevic', 'War's End', 'The Wise Teacher', 'The Bass Fishers', 'By Newport Station We Sat Down and Waited', 'What We Talk About When We Talk About Carver', 'An African Renaissance', 'Christmas in Cape Town', 'The Impossible Choice', 'Spoiled Idealism', 'On Spring Street' and 'Saving Private Daly'.

The BBC (From Our Own Correspondent) for 'Culture Shock in Chiantishire', 'Return to South Africa', 'A Boy Called "Grenade"', 'Farewell to Hong Kong', 'Wish You Were Here', 'A Tale of Two Dentists', 'The Rape of Michael Blucker' and 'Horror in the Mangroves'. All this material copyright © the BBC.

The Scotsman for 'Live and Let Dai'.

The Sunday Telegraph for 'A Raw Horse in the Mountains' and 'Seat of the Pants'.

The Guardian for 'The Boys of Summer'.

Time Magazine for 'Glad, So Glad to be Wrong'.

The author and publishers acknowledge permission to reproduce the following extracts: Raymond Carver, from 'Photograph of my Father in his Twenty-second Year', 'The Old Days', 'Hummingbird', 'Late Fragment', from All of Us: The Collected Poems, first published in Great Britain in 1996 by Harvill, © Tess Gallagher, 1996, reproduced by permission of The Harvill Press; Pablo Neruda, from 'They Come for the Islands', translated by W. S. Merwin, from Selected Poems, published in 1970 by Jonathan Cape, © the Estate of Pablo Neruda, reproduced by permission of

ACKNOWLEDGEMENTS

Random House Ltd; W. B. Yeats, from 'The Second Coming', reproduced by permission of A. P. Watt Ltd on behalf of Michael B. Yeats.

INTRODUCTION

I would like to introduce this collection by quoting from the work of the Russian poet Anna Akhmatova, one of my favourite writers. At the height of Stalin's terror the poet finds herself queuing outside a prison where her son is being held. She describes the numbed looks on the faces around her. They are mostly women, waiting to try and pass a parcel of food or clothes to the guards for their men. An old woman recognizes Akhmatova and approaches her. She asks the poet a simple question: 'Can you describe this?' And when Akhmatova answers that she can the old woman smiles. It is one of the most powerful moments in modern literature. For what Akhmatova is doing is making a promise that the terror will become part of the real history of her people. She will write, tell the stories, embed the executions and disappearances and jailings into the collective memory of her people. In clear, simple terms the poet described what I understand to be the central role of the journalist. To stand and say: *These things happened. Read them and remember them. These things happened.*

Akhmatova had genius. Most of us who roam the world reporting on its vicissitudes must work with a less powerful armoury. But however inelegant, however lacking in artfulness, words of witness *always* matter. Often they are all that is left us after the abandonment and betrayal of the powerful. There are some lines from St Teresa of Avila – quoted by the American poet Tess Gallagher – which I would like to repeat here: *words lead to deeds . . . they prepare the soul, make it ready, move it to tenderness.* The written and broadcast word can of course have precisely the opposite effect: from *Mein Kampf* to Rwanda's Radio Milles Collines our century has seen a horrible abundance of words which act, not as a spur to tenderness, but as agents of destruction. As a reporter in conflict zones I have often struggled to make a moral translation of the words I hear: the claims and the counterclaims, the speeches and press releases, the soundbites and interviews. I have not always succeeded. I have been lied to and have on occasion ended up believing lies. It happens in every journalistic life. With age and experience you end up, with luck, being less easy prey for the propagandists. But trying to separate the good from the bad, to make sense of places where black and white are too often smudged into grey, is always a challenge.

Too often, I believe, news reporting assumes a parity of plausibility – we set the claims of the oppressor alongside those of the victims in a manner that implies an equal level of believability. This is the journalism of 'on the one hand, on the other hand' and in the end it leaves us none the wiser as to the real truth of matters. Certainly the world is a complicated place. And it is unwise to fall into the trap of demonizing individuals or groups. But that does not mean we are obliged to fudge and obfuscate, to shy away from describing that which is evil as evil. Because there *are* bad guys and there are good guys. There are Nelson Mandelas and there are Slobodan Milosevics. The world is not an amoral swamp where people can be judged according to various levels of cynicism or nastiness.

I have always believed that what we do is about more than reporting the 'news', a swift and snappy recitation of the facts. Nor is it either solely a question of alerting the world to an immediate horror and, by implication at least, demanding action. It is also, critically, a matter of *recording* what happened, *who* made these things happen, *who* were the victims and *who* were the perpetrators. When you are an eyewitness to history – whether in Rwanda, the Balkans, Northern Ireland – there is an immense sense of privilege, and also a sobering feeling of responsibility. Because one event is so quickly overtaken by another, because we work in mediums of startling immediacy – the world of twenty-four-hour rolling news bulletins and the Internet – it is tempting to believe that what we say or write is quickly forgotten. The words themselves vanish before long, but the weight of those words, the truth they revealed or concealed, lasts long afterwards. As an example, let me quote the mis-reporting of the Rwandan genocide when newspapers like the New York Times and others spoke about irrational tribal violence and age-old enmities erupting into primitive savagery. The truth that this was a carefully planned campaign of extermination, only the second of its kind this century, was missed: to this day we are dealing with the consequences of this mis-reporting. I have lost count of the number of times I have heard journalists repeat those lazy and dangerous clichés which were chiselled into stone in the early days of the slaughter.

This collection includes a lengthy new piece ('Au Revoir, Mes Enfants') about returning to the Rwandan town of Butare for the first time since the genocide. There is also a series of letters from the Balkans as well as lighter and more personal pieces. It is a book of many journeys – from Sierra Leone to the mountains of Afghanistan, from the American mid-west to the farmland of North Kerry. Although much of my work concerns the terrors of life in zones of conflict, I would like to think my love of laughter also comes across in these pages. This collection is intended as a companion to Letter to Daniel – I hope I can succeed in bringing you with me into the exciting landscapes I've travelled through in the last years of the twentieth century.

My sincere thanks are due to Richard Sambrook and my other editors at the BBC who have given me the time to write and who've sent me to some of the world's most interesting places. Thanks are also due to Ian Burrell and the team at the Independent, where many of these pieces first saw the light of day; my gratitude also to Con Coughlin at the Sunday Telegraph, and to the Guardian and Time Magazine. Thanks to David Godwin, my agent, and Tony Lacey, my publisher. Tony Grant, the editor of From Our Own Correspondent, who takes much of the blame for encouraging me to write Letter to Daniel in the first place, was a key figure in the preparation of this volume. He knows how much he is valued. Above all, my love and thanks to Anne and Daniel, without whom life would not be life.

Part One

FROM CLOSE TO HOME

THE FUR TRAPPER

London, June 1999

Eamonn Patrick Keane died in 1990. His wife had left him long before and his son, the author of this book, had lost contact with him. He was an alcoholic and, his son thought, a fantasist. And yet, after his death, details emerged of his life as a young man in London which caused his son to think again.

All his life my father wanted to travel. He wanted to be a bold figure, an adventurer walking the high roads with nothing in his pockets. He dreamed of being the actor who charmed people in faraway places with his beautiful voice and his stories. In fact he wanted it so much he would imagine places he had been. I got used to these stories and though I did not believe him I would pretend that they were true. Things like that become a habit in relationships and I was always a good one for dreaming myself. You can dream yourself out of anywhere, no matter how small or painful a place it is. As far as I knew my father had been to England a couple of times, up to the North of Ireland a couple of times and that was the extent of his travelling.

Two years before his death my father came to visit me in Belfast where I was then working as a reporter. He had not been to the city since 1960 when he and my mother had been appearing in a play at the city's Opera House. They were only recently married and my mother was pregnant with me. By the time of my father's visit to me my parents had long since separated. My dad reminisced about that long distant stay in the city and asked me to drive him to north Belfast where he'd stayed with my mother in an old theatrical boarding house on Glencairn Avenue.

The house was gone now and the avenue had become one of the worst sectarian flashpoints in the city. But my dad remembered how the landlady – a legendary figure known as Mrs Burns – would serve them hearty Ulster fries late at night after the performances. He was wistful when he spoke for he knew the world he described – of generous theatrical landladies, of the great drama companies touring the towns of Ireland, of his own marriage and his youth – had long vanished. He told me how on their days off, he and my mother would roam about the city – it was still peaceful then, the explosion of the Troubles some eight years away. But my father tended not to talk too much about my mother and he only ever asked about her very tentatively. I think it was part guilt over the past, a great deal of inner pain (more than I ever understood) and some old-fashioned shyness too: it was not something he found easy to talk about. And so when he came to stay in Belfast we kept to safer ground. We mainly talked plays and politics and horse racing.

A man called Robbie who did odd jobs for the office took him on a tour of the city's Trouble spots. My father was fascinated by Belfast but horrified by the sectarianism that had carved the city into zones of tribal exclusion. Up the Falls and down the Shankill, across to the East and past the Shipyard, down the Ards Peninsula and back he questioned Robbie about 'the situation'.

It was during this trip that my father came up with his strangest imagined journey, a fantasy so bizarre I concluded that he had finally lost his grip on reality. It was the middle of winter and one of those days when the wind swept up the Lough and whipped at our faces. I was taking my father to meet Robbie in the city centre when I remarked on the cold. 'Ah yes,' my father nodded, 'it reminds me of my days with the Hudson Bay Trading Company. Bloody freezing it was.'

We were stopped at traffic lights. I didn't look at my father. I couldn't. I didn't know whether I should laugh or pretend to believe him. When the lights changed and we pulled away I snatched a glance. My dad was staring into the distance, staring deep into some imagined memory. 'You never smelt anything like the smell of those beaver skins. 'Twould make you sick it would,' he said. And I tried to imagine that. My father as a fur trapper on the banks of the Hudson River. Him and Lewis and Clarke and the Hurons and the Last of the Mohicans and great forests and snowy wastes. I thought about that and came to the conclusion that my dad had finally lost it. Soon afterwards he went back to Dublin. It was the last time he stayed with me. I gave up on him and his alcoholism sometime in the following year. Something in me gave out. I no longer called him and I gave up visiting.

The truth was that I felt past the point of rescues. There had been quite a few in the past ten years – a tour of detox hospitals, clinics and recovery wards. My father kept trying to live the straight life. The booze beat the daylights out of him but he kept trying. Once when he came out of hospital we went off and bought new clothes to celebrate. When he was sober he loved to dress in stylish clothes. This time he bought a sharp grey suit and fur-lined overcoat and two pairs of shoes and treated my wife and me to a meal in a Chinese restaurant. He really believed then, in those happy days after hospital, that he had beaten the drink. But like a terminal cancer it came back. Defeat after defeat piled up but the old man fought on. How hard it must have been, that struggle which went on and on. I try to imagine it but cannot. In the end I was the one who weakened, who could not take it and who said goodbye without ever telling him. I was the one whose endurance failed. And he was like a prize fighter too old for the ring, battered by the years, the man with the bruised face and the dazed look who kept getting up from the floor, who kept dodging and jabbing away. Memories:

I remember one summer finding an address for him in Dublin – this after a long period of silence between us – and going to visit him. He lived in a single room in an old house in Donnybrook in the south of the city. On the door there was a piece of faded brown paper which told visitors that they should knock three times for Mr Ryan, twice for Mr Singh and once for Mr Keane. I knocked once but there was no answer. A face appeared at an upstairs window, and an old man stared down at me. I knocked again and he came down. I explained who I was and that I wanted to leave a note. Mr Singh let me in and showed me to a room which overlooked the overgrown garden at the back. My father's clothes were everywhere. So were his papers and manuscripts. There were two gas rings for cooking, some food that had long gone stale and some empty whiskey bottles. On the table I saw a Bible lying open where he had finished reading it. I picked it up and saw that he had underlined the following words: 'Lord let me hear thy mercy in the morning, for I have hoped in thee.'

I stood there for a while and thought about that. Mercy in the morning. I have hoped in thee.

To think that he was still capable of hope. After all the defeats, he still hoped. I left a note for him and went away. My father kept moving. To a hospital around the corner from where he lived, to another one outside the city; to a centre run by a nun, to a room in the house of a kind woman who worked in the Abbey Theatre. And then as his health worsened there were emergency admissions to hospital, heart attacks that came close to killing him. I remember all of those hospitals and the extraordinary decency of those who took care of him. There was his brother John B. and his wife Mary, there was Andy the nurse at Vergemount Hospital in Dublin and Nicky Wilson, his neighbour in Donnybrook. Sweet, patient and loyal Nicky Wilson who never gave up on my dad, who was his friend to the very last. And there were other kinds of people who hung around him too. The cadgers of money and drink who zeroed in on him whenever a pay cheque arrived. I hated those drunks. To me they were parasites. I could not see that they too were addicts as desperate and trapped as him.

And then in the last year of his life I let go of my father. It was not a dramatic moment. I slipped slowly away from him. Once I was riding through Dublin on a bus and I caught sight of my dad in a crowded street. His hair needed cutting and he hadn't shaved for days. He had been drinking and looked as if he was in a lot of pain. But I kept going, I did not stop and jump off the bus to chase after him. My father vanished into the crowd, an old man weaving his way through a street filled with strangers.

Towards the end my father went home to Kerry, to the town where he was born. There his brother John B. and his family took care of him until he died at the age of sixty-five in early January, 1990. I was staying in Dublin at the time and my cousin rang with the news late one night. He simply said: 'He is gone.'

That was how it ended. There was no goodbye and no reconciliation. Not that my father would have criticized me for turning away from him in those last years. I know he would have smiled and told me not to worry. His death turned my world upside down. I loved him terribly and resented him bitterly. I blamed him for the pain of the past, for what he had not been, for the turmoil of those lost years of childhood. But if I am to tell you the truth I felt guilty too. For I had chosen to lose contact with him. When I got married I had not invited him to the wedding and I will never forget the humanity of his response: 'Don't worry, my love, these are only occasions, they don't affect anything.' The Christmas before he died I had not sent him a card. My wife had warned me that I would regret letting go of him when I was older. And I tried to explain that I was tired, that all of my life had been overshadowed by this impossible relationship, that I could not go on riding the emotional rollercoaster with my dad, that I was feeling half crazy myself let alone able to cope with his illness and pain. That was what I said.

And I did regret it later. I cannot write of him now or talk of those days without the tears streaming down my face, without a lump choking in my throat. It is so much unfinished business and the true writing of those times will have to wait until I can understand myself a great deal more clearly. I had wanted him to be somebody he could never be, I asked the impossible of him. He was a wounded man, filled with pain from the far-away past that I never understood and about which he could never really talk. Against all the evidence of the years I wanted him to be normal; I still believed I could turn him into the man who was like other fathers. I dreamed scenarios where he was 'cured' of his drinking and pain, where he would mellow into old age and be a grandfather to my children. At the age of thirty I still could not accept who my father was.

After he died I raced on into my own world. I became 'successful' and made a name. I had a son of my own and I wrote some things about my father's death and my own childhood. And I kept moving as far as I could from standing still and thinking. What I knew of my father was based on some hard memories and a lot of regret. It was a son's raw memory and it allowed for little in the way of outside views or different perspectives. My father the drunk, my father the fantasist – the man who spoke of gathering beaver skins for the Hudson Bay Trading Company – my father the lost man who appeared to me now in black and white, like a character from one of those old films he dreamed of acting in.

And then one evening last year the telephone rang and a man on the other end introduced himself as Paul and said he'd known my father many years ago in London. He was an artist now and lived in Bristol in retirement. Years ago he had big plans for becoming an actor and he met my dad when they were both looking for somewhere to stay in the city. 'I heard your voice and your name and wondered if you were his son,' said Paul. A few weeks later Paul came for dinner and over the course of four hours he told me stories of my father's life as a freelance actor in the London of the late 1950s.

I had no knowledge of this life before now. I knew that there had been an incident in Ireland around 1957 when my father had insulted a government minister at a public function and had had to leave the country in a hurry. When my father arrived in England he had few, if any, contacts and made his way around the theatre companies and the London agents. Somewhere along the way he

8

ran into Paul Piercy, who had come up from the West Country looking for acting work. They found a room in Chelsea but there was little in the way of work. 'We had high hopes and great energy, I think your father believed he could have done anything at that time, that the world was going to open up before him and make him a star,' remembered Paul.

To pay the rent the two young men went looking for odd jobs. Among the first was a season spent picking hops in Kent along with hundreds of families from the East End. Paul remembered it as hard work but said my father loved listening to the voices and accents of the people in the fields. He was terrified of the women though. 'I think he thought all those English girls were a bit wild and that they would jump on him. They weren't like the women at home in Kerry. Whenever we met any on the road he would want to cross to the other side.' Near the end of their time in the hop fields, they were sleeping in a barn with gypsies and Paul remembered a fantastic thunderstorm with lightning flashing across the sky all night.

A lot of the time the money they earned was spent on drink. 'Even then I sensed something was not happy with your father. The way he drank, how he lost control once he started. There were a lot of scrapes and times when he would disappear for a few days and come back in an awful condition. But he was generous when he had the money and patient with his time, so patient with his time. I was never going to be a professional actor, it was your father who was the talented one. But he would spend hours with me going over parts, trying to teach me the art of the thing, rehearsing me through my lines. And I know that is maybe not what you experienced growing up, that he was not around for you. But he did try and help me and give me his time and I will never forget him for it.'

Once my father had taken him to meet Samuel Beckett in the George Pub near Broadcasting House. Paul didn't know how my father came to meet Beckett originally but he said the literary giant had been kind and generous to them. 'Your father made him laugh which wasn't what people tended to expect of Beckett.' They had met Louis MacNeice as well after my father found some work at the BBC where the poet was a senior producer.

And then I asked what other jobs they had done. Paul paused and thought for a moment. There was one extraordinary job, he said, something they had only done when there was no other way of getting the money. In those days there was a big warehouse in Covent Garden where the Hudson Bay Trading Company stored huge amounts of furs imported from the far north of Canada. If you didn't fancy breaking your back on the building sites you could go down there and try for piece work. 'We went down there a few times and got jobs sorting out the skins. It was beaver skins and other stuff like that. It was bloody cold in that place and the smell from those things was rotten. We would go into the pub afterwards and people would move away from us, we smelt that bad. But it was money and we couldn't afford to turn it down.'

I sat back from the table. The Hudson Bay Trading Company. Beaver skins that stank. I was taken aback. So my father had been telling the truth on that grey morning back in Belfast. I didn't know what to make of that information, where it would fit into the way I saw my dad. But I felt a twinge of shame for having refused to believe him. And as I sat at the table a picture formed in my mind: my father with his hair dark and wild and his eyes full of romance and passion; my father on the streets of London proclaiming his lines aloud to his soulmate Paul Piercy, the crowds staring at them and they not caring a damn; my father with the future still glittering before him, a young man trembling with hope. And now when I see him in my mind's eye it is that picture I try to cling to – of the man before defeat, before the disaster that engulfed him and those who loved him.

Before he left my house Paul Piercy said he had a present for my young son. He opened his bag and took out a heavy old book, *The Complete Works of William Shakespeare*, published by Spring Books of London. On the flyleaf there was the following inscription: 'To Paul from Eamonn – with best wishes for a happy 100th birthday.' Paul told me that my father had given him the book as a birthday present in November 1958. And now he was returning it to me, so that Eamonn's grandson might read it someday and remember the young actor who had sorted stinking furs for the Hudson Bay Company so he could rent a room to rehearse his lines. Somewhere to keep his dreams alive.

IN THE HEART OF
THE COUNTRY

London, June 1999

The author enjoys a career which often takes him far from his native Ireland: to Africa and Asia and to many other worldwide locations, some glamorous but all of them memorable. But he never forgets the images and even the smells associated with his childhood. Of particularly fond memory is a period spent in North Kerry. This was a time before prosperity arrived in Ireland, when the rest of the world seemed a great distance away, and Irish people were still held in the iron grip of the church.

My first country memory is of an afternoon in high summer and me riding with my cousin Willie Purtill on a donkey and cart along a laneway thick with fuchsia and brambles. I must have been about six years old and we were returning from the creamery at Lisselton on the main road between my father's town, Listowel, and the seaside village of Ballybunnion. An empty milk churn sat between us and Willie tapped his fingers methodically on the metal casing. His other hand held the reins and from time to time he clicked his tongue, a reminder to the ancient and slow-moving donkey that we were depending on him to get us home. Around us the farmland of North Kerry stretched from Cnoc on Oir (the Mountain of Gold) down to the Atlantic Ocean at Ballybunnion, a wide stretch of land where the pasture is interspersed with snipe grass and the dark loam of the bogs. It was now the first week of the harvest and we could smell the aromas of new-mown hay and ripening blackberries mingling with the sea salt that drifted in from the Atlantic.

This was the territory of my grandmother Hannie's people. She was my father's mother and it was said that her people – the

Purtills – had come over from Spain in the last century. The name apparently is a derivation of Portillo, from which knowledge you are free to cast any aspersion you wish. They were people with a great gift for laughter and 'blaggarding'. The latter term can be used to describe a wide variety of behaviour including an excessive attraction to drink, horses, cards or women – or any combination of the aforementioned.

To a young city boy the Purtills were the most welcoming people imaginable. The family farm at Lisselton – the name itself rings with magic – was a garden of mystery. Here I was shown how to milk a cow by hand (this was the time before milking parlours), the warm milk spraying across my sandals while old Madge Purtill clucked away behind me. 'Aim for the bucket, boy, aim for the bucket. God, we'll make a farmer of you yet.' I never mastered the art. It was here too that I ran after men as they forked huge piles of hay on to the carts, chased the farm dogs and cats, and tormented my cousin Willie to take me with him to the creamery.

Willie was a gentle big fellow and hugely tolerant of my pestering. On the morning that I remember most vividly we had travelled half the journey home when we reached a thatched building and Willie pulled hard on the reins to stop the donkey. 'Wait here a while, boyo,' he said to me. He disappeared into the dark interior of the building from where I could hear men's voices laughing. After a few minutes Willie returned with a tin mug filled to the brim with a foaming black substance. 'Would you like a sup of porter?' he asked. 'What's porter?' I replied. 'It's a kind of drink,' he said. I lifted the mug and took a long gulp of warm, bitter liquid. They say that most children hate the taste of alcohol. But I loved it. I felt as if I was going to float off over the hedgerows. 'What do you think?' he asked. 'It's nice,' I responded. 'Good man, good man,' said Willie, patting me on the back. Thus did I make the acquaintance of Guinness.

The countryside of those days was still relatively unspoilt. Those were the days before 'bungalow bliss' and the unlovely ranch-style houses which ruined so much of Ireland's rural landscape. I was an early convert to the magic of the Irish countryside. Back then it was still a place in thrall to old traditions and mythologies. The power of the Catholic Church was absolute but beneath the cloak of puritan morality lurked older, more elemental forces. I had a clear sense that my Kerry ancestors were sensual, wild people upon whom the strictures of narrow morality did not sit easily. They loved good music, strong drink and sex. It was the job of the priests to subdue these impulses – and in doing so they often twisted and perverted what was natural and good. Sex became the 'deed done in darkness' – a fit pastime for making God's babies but not for pleasure. But much though the church might have scowled and warned, the pagan heart kept beating.

Once during a priestly mission there was a loud denunciation of 'cheek to cheek' dancing, which had begun to enjoy widespread popularity in the area. My father – then a teenager – had declined to go to the mission and had been upbraided in the street by a priest. I treasure his reply: 'Father, your fulminations here will have as much effect on the populace as would the flatulence of a blackbird on the water levels of the Grand Coulee Dam.' The priest, staggered by this jumble of images, walked away muttering to himself.

The greatest of all passions in that country was for land. Men judged their worth by the acre – it was more than the money of course, much deeper. The self-esteem of a man and his family, in a real sense their belief in themselves, was rooted in the ownership of this field and that. Often the farmer's love of his land was greater than any love he might have for woman or child. My uncle John B once described watching a farmer tenderly running his fingers through ears of corn on a late summer day. 'It was like seeing a man run his hands through the hair of a beautiful woman,' he said. Men killed for the love of land and no power on earth or in heaven would dare come between them and the loam of a North

Kerry field. In a powerful play later turned into a Hollywood movie, John B wrote of a notorious case where one neighbour had murdered another in a dispute over land – the writing of the play brought death threats to my uncle for years after the event.

In this modern age of factory farming and Brussels bureaucracy it might be hard to appreciate such a deep-rooted attachment to the land. But these were people for whom famine was a living memory: they lived in an area where half the population had been wiped out by hunger within the previous century. Land was not something to be thrown away or left idle. I sometimes wonder what those farmers of my grandparents' generation would feel about the vast acres left idle under the EU's agriculture policies. Disgust and bewilderment, I suspect.

But that is a digression from the journey of memory. What else comes back from those long-ago summers? I remember the beach at Ballybunnion where the tinkers sold snacks of dried seaweed and periwinkles and where Mrs Collins' seaweed baths were the best-known cure for all diseases. You filled the bath of hot water with lumps of local seaweed and then waited until it became a glutinous mess before luxuriating in it for an hour. Afterwards you ran down the beach and jumped into the icy waves and, suitably mortified, ran back to Mrs Collins' little café where she supplied ham sandwiches and hot tea.

It was in Ballybunnion that I first rode a horse. I use 'rode' in the most loose of senses. The memory is seared into my consciousness. It started out ordinarily enough. A small fat man – a 'maneen' in the local vernacular – led the horse sedately across the beach. But halfway through the ride my younger cousin Conor came creeping up behind the poor animal and smacked it hard on the rump. The horse took off at a fierce gallop in the direction of the cliffs. I could see a hard wall of black rock facing me and the terrorized animal rushing headlong towards destruction. It was halted only by an extraordinary bellow from its owner, who had come running after us. I howled and was treated to a candy floss. My cousin had his ears boxed.

My father's people were master story-tellers. They were the inheritors of a rich oral tradition, of a language and way of speaking which grew out of the marriage of Gaelic and of Elizabethan English. It was both richly poetic and capable of masterful vagueness. How many times did I hear growing up that a Kerryman always answers a question with a question. For example: an American tourist stops at a crossroads in North Kerry and asks where he might find the post offfice. The local who is idling at the crossroads replies: 'Is it stamps you want?' They were – it goes without saying – an innately curious people.

At nights on holidays we listened to ghost stories in my grandmother's kitchen. It was a traditional country kitchen with an open range which served as both fire and cooker. In the old days the neighbours would come in to play cards and to dance and tell stories. My father was a gifted teller of tall tales. He mixed the big Irish legends with local folklore and we listened wide-eyed with fright as the country night drew down in shadows around us. His favourite story was about a British officer who my father said had been shot dead in front of my grandmother's house. According to the story the officer had been walking home from mass when he was ambushed and shot by the IRA outside Hannie's front door. My father used to say that a green shadow, the ghost of the soldier, passed across the walls in the deep reaches of the night. 'If ye stay awake, ye'll see it,' he said. We always fell asleep though. Years later I heard that an inspector from the Royal Irish Constabulary had been murdered on the street on his way home from mass. But my grandmother and father were dead by this time and I had no way of checking if this was the man my father had spoken of.

Sitting around that kitchen as a child I heard many stories of dead relatives. One grand-uncle was reputed to have gone to a cattle mart with a pound note pinned to his jacket. When asked why he had done this, he replied: ''Tis to show them all I'm a man of substance.' These were people with a living memory of the most dire poverty and hunger, and hunger meant shame and degradation. Little wonder a man could take such almighty pride in what he owned. What you had you held on to and were proud of.

Later on those feelings would manifest themselves in a fierce determination to get a good education, to get up to Dublin or Cork and go to college. My grandmother Hannie's greatest pride was reserved for good exam results. Whether it was sons, grandsons, nephews or nieces she kept a sharp eye on their academic progress. Education was the way up, a degree a badge of pride for the whole family.

Her husband Bill Keane was a quiet man who couldn't have cared less about the wealth of the world or what others thought of him. He was a schoolteacher and every morning he walked twelve miles to the little school at Clounmacon, outside Listowel. He did it in winter snow and in summer heat. My grandfather's great mistake was not to play up to the priests who ruled the roost at the time. He was an independent-minded man, one who loved books and knowledge and loathed the cant that was shoved down people's throats at mass and mission services. But he paid a price for his independence – no promotion, no move to a school nearer home and the priests breathing down his neck relentlessly. He was also strongly attracted to drink and I know this caused friction in the house from time to time. But it was a small part of a man who was remembered by his pupils (two of them contacted me last summer) as warm and generous with his time and knowledge. He died when I was two years old after battling with cancer of the throat.

But I am wandering too far from those lanes of North Kerry and the images and smells which come back of those days. You always knew you had arrived in my father's country when you smelled the turf-smoke on the air. It hit you somewhere near Tarbert on the Shannon estuary and continued all the way from the coast to the town. And I can vividly recall too the smell of smoked bacon in Toddy Connor's shop across the street from my grandmother's. Toddy had a big countryman's face with twinkling eyes and greeted you always as if he had not seen you in decades. He sold huge lumps of meat and vast quantities of spuds and cabbage. I remember him mainly as a good man to cadge sweets from.

If I am truthful, though, it is the physical landscape of those Kerry summers with which I formed the strongest bond. There was Gurtenard Wood, which my father told us was filled with bears and foxes and wolves, the Feale River with its deep pools, the Knight of Kerry's castle (an old Elizabethan-era ruin), the beaches at Ballybunnion and the mysterious barn at the end of my grandmother's garden. This old brick building was piled high with turf, under which we were convinced lay chests full of Elizabethan treasure. Of course we never dug under the turf. That, we sensed, might have spoiled the illusion.

As I grew older so North Kerry changed. It became a great deal more prosperous and the church lost its iron grip on the hearts and minds of the people. The local farmers set up a co-operative which became one of Europe's richest agricultural operations. There were factories opening in nearby Tralee and along the estuary of the River Shannon to the west. In my teenage years Listowel was where I went to indulge my growing appetite for porter and young women. To subsidize my adventures I worked part-time in my uncle John B.'s bar. He and his wife Mary were the most generous employers under the sky.

One of the greatest rewards of working with them, though, was listening to the extraordinary cast of characters who floated through the pub every day. The most formidable of the summer regulars was Jimmy Boylan. Although he came from the alien territory of Cork city – eighty miles or so away – Boylan enjoyed the status of honoured guest. My uncle was like that with people: if they did him a good turn, showed his family kindness, he would never forget them. Boylan had been kind in the past and was rewarded with his special place at the bar. The Corkman carried with him many prejudices; most notable of these was a lifelong hatred for Henry Ford, the automobile maker. Boylan had worked at the Ford plant in Cork for many years and believed that he had been exploited terribly. The very mention of the name Ford was enough to produce a vicious tirade – and naturally we mentioned the name as often as we could. 'Wasn't Ford a great car maker? Wasn't Ford a great employer?' etc., etc.

The most mysterious of the characters who frequented John B.'s public house was Davy Gunn, the maker of bodhrans, the handheld drums used in traditional Irish music. He was a man who spoke little but when he did speak you listened to every well-chosen word. He once paused in his drinking to tell me that tadpoles were the bane of his life. They haunted the water where he treated the goatskin that was used to make the bodhrans, nibbling away at the precious material until it was useless. 'Bad bastarding hoors,' he said.

The bar work subsidized my growing interest in women and drink. My teacher in these matters was my cousin Conor – the one who had slapped the horse's backside all those years before in Ballybunnion. As a teacher he was patient – devoting whole nights to showing me how many pints of Guinness could be consumed before one felt the urge to run to the toilet and vomit. We went to a great many dances but I don't ever remember either of us 'striking out' with any of the local girls. Conor gave the impression that he couldn't care less. I gave the impression that I cared too much. I did once manage to persuade a girl to go 'down to the strand' but when I tried to recite poetry to her, she looked at me as if I was a madman. 'Will you f—k away off and get on with it,' she said. I was shattered and retreated. Conor was waiting for me with a knowing smile when I climbed up from the beach. 'You can always trust your pint,' he said, smirking.

I still go back to North Kerry as often as I can. John B.'s pub and home is as welcoming as ever. It is my father's country and my country too. There was a lot of pain in that world and I have written about some of that in other places. But there was much laughter and a great deal of love too. And I admit to a great pride in the contrariness of the people, their flashes of defiance and their delight in mischief. As my aunt Mary – who married into the family – once put it: 'They're wild hoors, those Keanes. You have to keep a close eye on them.'

ROCK 'N' ROLL DAYS

Cork, June 1999

Rory Gallagher wasn't Cork's only rock star. Anyone who attended his gigs in Ardmore, at the Cork Boat Club or the Cricket Club dance, would surely have agreed that superstardom was just around the corner for young Fergal Keane. But then again, they might have had something much more offensive to say!

My guitar teacher looked at me with pity. We had just spent an hour on the 'House of the Rising Sun' and my singing was getting worse. 'Son, you might make a guitar player, but I'd give up the singing if I was you,' he said. He was a droll Canadian who gave tuition to aspirant rock stars like myself in an attic room near St Peter and Paul's Church. The maestro explained that not everybody was cut out to be a singer. Guitar playing was something that you could improve with practice. But a bad voice was like having no voice. You just couldn't create sounds that weren't there. 'Damn you,' I said (to myself) and got up to leave. Sensing that this might be a final moment of sorts the Canadian reminded me that I still owed him sixteen quid for the guitar. I promised that I would be back for a lesson the following week along with his money. I never returned and I never paid. If you are out there Mr Teacher please get in touch. That sixteen quid is burning a hole in my pocket and my conscience.

My confidence might have taken a bit of a bruising but I had three things in my favour: I had a guitar, I could play at least three chords and I had an ego the size of a football field. For an aspirant rock star in the city of Cork these were not inconsiderable assets. In those days we teenagers were living under enemy occupation. They were everywhere. The Army of the Republic of NO: the priests and the teachers and the parents and the politicians, the

GAA men and – still clinging on – the cultural commissars holding to their dream of a Gaelic Ireland, the whole boring bloody lot of them keeping us in check . . . but only barely. For the Ireland of my adolescence was being convulsed with strange new forces, we sensed we were standing on the cusp of a revolution and wanted to be part of it. The sixties had been and gone and shaken things up. But the hippies had grown up and got married. Men we had admired for their long hair and contempt for authority had gone off to become teachers and doctors. They had swapped their tie-dyes and bell bottoms for tweed jackets and slacks.

By the middle of the 1970s I was lurching into adolescence and preparing myself for revolution. Strange sounds erupted in the night, rupturing the drone of adult voices. Deep under the blankets I twirled the dials until the voice of freedom rang out. Luxembourg Calling, Luxembourg Calling and the voice of Tony Prince with the 208 Power Play. 'Who the hell is Tony Prince?' a friend of mine asked one day. Like me he listened every night. But I couldn't help him. 'Some flash bastard with a big yellow sportscar and a rake of women hanging off him,' I said. I then told my friend that the person himself didn't matter. It was the music that set you free. 'That sounds like a load of old shite,' said my friend. He was right.

A few weeks after that I went up to stay with friends in Dublin and asked them what they thought of Tony Prince and Radio Luxembourg. The eldest son of the family threw his eyes up to heaven. 'Tony Prince is for wankers and kids. You want to listen to Radio Caroline.'

And so I switched to Caroline and migrated from the glam rock of 208 to the likes of Pink Floyd and Yes and Genesis. That was the summer I grew my hair and began to see myself as a major star of the future. It was also the summer I went to my first live gig. It was modern jazz and the most boring load of tripe I had ever heard. But my sophisticated friends loved it. And naturally I agreed. But I was glad to get back to Cork. Down south the music was a lot more raw. After all Cork was the home of Rory Gallagher, prince of the blues. Cork City Hall was where he played every Christmas – a long-haired hero in check shirt who sent us home with our ears ringing and the clothes sticking to our backs.

I didn't get involved with a band until I was midway through secondary school. A friend of mine called Chris Ahern was also a big rock fan and a promising guitarist. Chris loved the Beatles, especially the early rhythm and blues numbers. His eldest brother was one of the top guitarists on the local scene and the family home was filled with music of all kinds. Since coming back from my summer in Dublin I had developed an addiction to the Rolling Stones and practised my Jagger impersonations in front of the bedroom mirror every night. We had a wealthy schoolfriend called Ger who allowed us to practise in his house. He was the only one with a decent instrument – a mahogany bass guitar – and was naturally guaranteed a place in the band. We found a drummer at school and began to rehearse a set of Beatles and Stones numbers. Our first name was 'Home Brew' but I can't remember why. Then we graduated to 'The Runners' (we had a symbol of a tennis shoe on our home-drawn posters) and finally 'The Streets'.

I can't remember our first gig. Probably out of shame. We were pretty crap in the beginning. It wasn't until my brother Eamonn came along that the music started to pick up. He was a trained musician who could take his hand to any instrument and make it sing. He took over on bass and along with Chris started to impose some kind of musical discipline. What was my own role in this grand enterprise? So much for the droll Canadian's warnings . . . I was the *lead* singer.

Our first triumph was a charity hop at school. By now we had shifted our rehearsal rooms to the children's nursery, which was run by Chris's mother. Her tolerance was boundless as we pounded out one rock classic after another. By the time the gig came around we were, as they say in the business, a 'tight' unit. Such a night of glory. The crowd – mostly our friends – jumped and hopped and gave us three encores. I had flung myself around the stage with fierce abandon, my ego firing on all cylinders. The band were so loud that I'm not sure the audience heard much of what I sang. It was the beat that mattered – a truth I would never forget.

We began to pick up gigs around the city. At the Arcadia – where U2 played (imagine that!) – we played to a big crowd; biggish at any rate. There was Shandon Boat Club and Cork Boat Club and the Cricket Club dance. For the latter we were forced to broaden our range and include 'pop' songs. We were tormented by members of the audience wanting to sing and use us as a backing band. The gigs were not always triumphs and my ego was frequently dented. We had no money and were reduced to borrowing and begging equipment. Sometimes the gear was good, but often it made us sound like we were playing inside a washing machine. For transport we usually depended on one of our mothers. I remember once the entire band plus equipment and my baby brother being packed into my mother's Mini for a forty-mile trip. (We were skinny young lads.)

The best gig I can remember was in Ardmore, where my family went for the summer holidays every year. The local hall was called St Declans and I had enjoyed my first dances under its tin roof. Most of the bands who came there were regulars on the country and western circuit. 'The Antelopes' (I am serious), 'The Double Units' (twin sisters), 'The Indians' (complete with tribal gear) were a few of the big names who came. It wasn't my type of music but they were genuine professionals. No bum notes, no whining feedback, no forgetting the words. None of the diseases from which we in 'The Streets' suffered so regularly. But our Ardmore gig was a hit. As usual we had taken the precaution of stacking the audience with friends and family. But there was something about the venue – the heat, the abandon of summer, the patchouli perfume and the testosterone – which lifted us from being averagely good into one moment of greatness . . . well, for me at least.

Afterwards there was the usual row about money with the parish priest. They were the hardest men in Ireland to deal with. You would have had more luck getting money from the Sicilian Mafia than one of the reverend fathers. Once when we were denied our share of the takings we decided a symbolic protest was in order. And so – as the crowds were leaving – we returned to the stage and began to play a punk number. We jumped and jumped and pounded and went crashing through the floorboards. Viva rock 'n' roll.

Looking back it was some of the best fun I've ever had. Soon enough the dreams of glory departed and I played purely for the fun . . . and the gratification of my ego. Oh that beautiful cheering! It didn't bring streams of groupies to the dressing-room door. I had a regular girlfriend who would have taken a dim view of all that. And besides I suspect many of the girls who came to our gigs thought me a little insane – it was fine watching Mick Jagger on TV, but there was something unsettling about seeing Micky the Mope from up the road gyrating and thrusting in front of you.

One of our last gigs was at a rural harvest festival – a dance held at the end of the harvesting – near a seaside town on the County Cork coast. It ended in chaos when a crowd of Dutch fishermen arrived and took over the stage. Later that night there was a big fight with the locals and – *quelle surprise* – the priest couldn't find the money to pay us exactly what we were owed. Our driver was a notorious hard man in Cork and asked me if I wanted him to negotiate with the priest. I took one look at Micky and decided this would be unnecessary. Micky was shot dead in a drugs war in Cork years later.

By the time we left school the band was in the process of disintegrating. The real musicians like my brother and Chris were exploring different styles and writing their own material. I was never more than an amateur with a half-decent voice. When I left to become a newspaper reporter in another city, we played together only sporadically.

Both Eamonn and Chris went on to become accomplished and highly regarded musicians – and I sang at parties whenever anybody asked. It wasn't until I moved to South Africa that the call of the stage returned in the person of a British diplomat named Michael Shipster. I'd met Shippo at a party and we got to talking about music. In a few minutes we'd set up a guitar session and the rest is history. Well, sort of. South African history at any rate.

In the closing days of the white empire Johannesburg was a city of never-ending parties where people were only too happy to dance away their worries. Shippo and I saw the potential opening and formed a band. Our drummer was a cameraman for German TV, our bass player a sound recordist. In mockery of a phrase from the anti-communist paranoia of the apartheid years we called the band 'Total Onslaught'. We were hot. Very hot. We played about four gigs but I am sure South Africa has never forgotten them. The final epic performance came at the time of the first multi-racial election. The week after the votes were cast and the new ANC government came to power, we performed to a crowd of journalists and politicians in the lush premises of the Transvaal Automobile Club. The new deputy Minister of Defence, Ronnie Kasrils (a famous anti-apartheid activist), joined us on stage to sing and dance.

The occasion was marred only when my instructions to our pianist – the BBC's veteran Zimbabwe correspondent Ian Mills – were picked up by the microphone. I had just asked one of the guitarists to play a solo when Millsy misheard the instruction and turned up his piano, blaring away over everybody else. 'Not you, you idiot,' I shouted angrily. The audience erupted into laughter and Millsy looked crestfallen. I hope he has forgiven me. It was a great night in the middle of extraordinary times.

Since then I have only played guitar at home, waiting for a phone call that I suspect will never come. My rock 'n' roll days are probably over and I never became a star. But what the hell – it was only rock 'n' roll and I liked it, I loved it. Yeah, yeah, yeah.

THE BASS FISHERS

Sierra Leone, March 1999

Another troublespot and more reporting tales of horror and violence. But then, when the work is done, a chance to daydream; to think of home, to savour friendships and memories of afternoons spent fishing for giant salmon, tiny trout and the great Atlantic bass.

I am travelling in one of the world's darker corners right now, but more of that another time. On this weekend, heavy with international gloom, I am taking up the editor's generous invitation to write about what I want to. And what I want to write about is hidden rivers and Atlantic beaches and the fish that haunt them – the places that Raymond Carver described as those where 'water comes together with other water'.

If I close my eyes right now I can shut out the night sounds of an African city – jangling guitars, shouts of joy and of violence – and imagine that I hear the water lisping on the stones of Ballyquinn on a night at the end of August. To fish is to let go of the hustle of life, it is about finding your own space and doing nothing much but watching tide and current and waiting hopefully for the magical twitch at the end of the rod.

I don't fish enough these days but I daydream about it a great deal. Living in London means a long drive to the coast, battling the motorway traffic and arriving tired and snappish and probably catching nothing.

My problem is that I don't know these English waters, the right places to fish, the proper bait to use, any of the local lore so essential to success (or so the locals always insist). Such a journey would only end up in the pub, swapping fishing stories with other bores like myself. There's nothing wrong with that, but I at least like to feel that I have had a go at hooking a fish.

27

This earnestness in the matter of fish is something that comes from my childhood. Back then I lived for fishing. I studied all the books I could find, spent my pocket money on angling magazines and tormented my parents to take me to the sea or the river. My first fishing memory is in County Kerry at about the age of six. I can still remember the magic of light on water on the River Feale and my father playing a small baited line back and forth in a deep pool. He told me there were huge salmon lurking below, creatures so big they could drag a man to his death in minutes.

I was suitably awed and waited . . . and waited. We were there for several hours and I had started to give up hope, and then my father let out a shout of joy. We had a fish. A fish! For the first time in my life a fish. My father pulled the line in with suspiciously little effort. As our catch came into the shallows he handed it over to me. With heart pounding I continued to pull. But even with a six-year-old's puny arms I had no difficulty with this specimen, a tiny brown trout that wriggled and splashed on the surface.

I think my father suggested throwing him back but I would have none of it. I wanted to take the thrawneen (an Irish word for something stunted or tiny) home for my grandmother to cook in her big kitchen on Church Street. And so we marched home through Gurtenard Wood and across the square and then up Church Street. I remember that it was not yet dark, only a few lights twinkled in the houses and shops and pubs we passed. People were standing on the street chatting, and my father stopped to talk to every one of them. That was his style. He gave every man and woman the time of day while I displayed my fish with great pride.

That was way back in the 1960s, and I had big plans for fishing with my dad. For one reason and another they did not work out, and as I got older I attached myself to a series of patient older men who taught me the art of fishing. Two stand out in particular: John Ryan, a schoolteacher from Dublin, and Eric Malley, his friend from County Tyrone. I think the word patience understates the kindness they showed me. They steered me through the agonies of endless tangled lines and through the long nights when nothing was biting. I met them in Ardmore, where my family spent the summer holidays. They were both committed sea anglers, loving the freedom of the wide beaches and the crash of Atlantic surf.

Night after August night we would pile into John Ryan's old black Rover and head for one beach or another along the West Waterford coast: Ballyquinn, Whiting Bay, Caliso, Curragh Strand, Ardmore beach. I am sure I tormented the poor men, but only once did they try to leave me behind. It was a night they had planned to spend drinking at Fleming's bar above Ballyquinn beach (their wives having been told they were taking young Keane out to fish). But it wasn't easy to give the slip to an obsessive like me. As the two were heading up the main street to the car, I appeared in front of them, rod in hand. With their wives watching they had no option but to bring me along. We did not fish; I was given a bottle of Powers lemonade and a bag of crisps and allowed to sit beside them as they drank Bosuns (the West Waterford name for a large bottle of Guinness) and told yarns.

Through watching their skill on the beach I slowly turned into a half-decent fisherman, even winning a flashlight in the Modern Kitchens annual beach competition. It was a big ignorant red flashlight but I was the proudest boy in Ardmore that night.

If you fish that coast for any length of time and listen to the locals you will learn that there really is only one fish worth catching, the Atlantic bass. The toughest fighter in our coastal waters and the nicest fish to eat bar none. I never feel a summer is complete without at least one bass on the end of the line. In the old days – that's the 1970s – we hauled them in by the dozen. On one memorable night on Ballyquinn the Ryans – John and his fishing fanatic son Stan – hauled in something in the region of thirty fish . . . or was it fifty?

At the age of fourteen I discovered girls in a serious way and drifted away from fishing. But it was only a temporary parting. I came back to the beaches in my late teens. The girls could let you down but the sand and sea and the stars that frosted our late August skies . . . well they would last for ever. And every summer since, I have made the time to fish. Last summer John Ryan, older now and not as fit as he once was, took me and Stan and his grandsons to a beach I had forgotten about, a place that could only be reached with a long climb over black and threatening rocks. John did not follow us, preferring to sit on an old stone bridge and contemplate the sea. I imagined he was thinking of those other days when he led us all across rocks and dunes, our leader and hero and the wisest fisherman in West Waterford.

I am already training my son to fish; at three years of age he is still somewhat terrified by the flapping and jumping of the landed fish. But whenever I mention fishing he wants to go with me, and I take that as an encouraging sign. Some day soon he will be tugging on my jacket, pulling me out of some soft armchair and calling out those place names: Ballyquinn, Whiting, Curragh, Ardmore, Caliso. Places a fisherman should go.

THE WISE TEACHER

London, January 1999

**There are some teachers who are best forgotten, and others whose
influence lives on long after school days are over. Brother Jerome,
who had to educate an obnoxious young Keane, proved to
be an inspiration.**

I don't know why I think you might be interested in the story of
a teacher who came from a small rural community on the stormy
south-west coast of Ireland. It could be that you will get to the
end of this story and feel it was a waste of time. I hope not. The
story of Jerome Kelly is about bigger things than where he came
from, who he taught, the lives he changed. Sure they were important. But they were by-products and not the central idea which
governed the life now gone.

I was an awkward thirteen-year-old when I first met him. To
the new pupils like myself he was Brother Jerome, the headmaster
who strode down our gleaming corridors, his black robes billowing
behind him like the wings of some great bird of prey. In those
early days we feared him. The man had serious presence. When
he approached, you stopped fidgeting and fool acting. You stood
up straight and listened to what he had to say.

But after a few days we noticed that Jerome had yet to hit
anyone. In the Ireland of those days teachers regularly beat the
children in their care. They were the days of the leather and the
cane, the chalk duster and the fist. The Christian brothers were the
most notorious of the physical-force men – the military wing of
the Catholic Church. The prevailing attitude was that a good beating
never did anyone any harm. But Jerome, we learned, did not
operate like that. He was a Presentation Brother, a group with a
reputation for being slightly more gentle.

I never saw Jerome raise his hand to a boy. He didn't need to. Although he was a short man, Brother Jerome radiated authority. I ran into that authority frequently during my first few years in secondary school. I suppose the psychologists would say I was looking for attention – talking in class, trying to be funny, practical jokes.

On the first occasion I was dispatched to the headmaster's office, Jerome eyed me balefully. 'Come back when school is over, boy,' he growled. My comrade-in-crime was another talkative youth, Michael Kiernan, who would later win fame as a rugby international playing with Ireland and the British Lions.

Jerome's idea of punishment was to send the two of us out on to the city streets with black bin bags. When we returned several hours later, dragging the bin bags behind us, Jerome was waiting with a smile. 'You have repaid your debt to society, gentlemen,' he said. All of his punishments were like that. There was always a point. Cleaning up rubbish, staying back after school to study a book on civic responsibility, writing an essay on why we misbehaved.

I got into a lot of trouble after that. Nothing serious but a steady stream of incidents: helping to smuggle a vicious terrier into class (the terrified animal bit left, right and centre); conspiring to stuff a dead bird into the case of a particularly boring teacher; and talking, always talking. I was an obnoxious little clown.

Instead of cracking down, Jerome took a different tack. He insisted that I join the school debating society. 'Put your talking skills to some positive use, boy.' The debating opened up a new world to me. I found I could stand in front of people and hold their attention. Jerome ferried us around the country to debating competitions in freezing convent halls. Ireland was opening up then and Jerome encouraged us to speak about the issues that mattered to us as teenagers.

I am sure that we horrified a few reverend mothers with our outspoken rants on the ills of Irish society. But Jerome backed us all the way. Midway through our third year, he introduced philosophy classes. These were to run in conjunction with the obligatory religious instruction. But in an overwhelmingly Catholic country the idea of introducing philosophy lessons, of opening our minds to Russell and Wittgenstein, was revolutionary.

'Think boys, think. Use your minds,' he would say.

The school was famous in Ireland. 'Pres College' was traditionally a school for the sons of the city's merchant princes. In the days of the British empire, it produced civil servants for the colonies. It encouraged the games of cricket and rugby, especially rugby. In many senses 'Pres' was a conscious imitation of the English public school.

By the time Jerome arrived as headmaster, the school had lost much of its academic lustre. The joke was that it had become a little like a basin of clotted cream – filled with the rich and thick. Jerome came to 'Pres' by way of the West Indies, where he had been working as a missionary. In those newly independent territories, he had thrown himself with gusto into the task of educating a new generation of leaders. Many of the ministers and judges of post-colonial Trinidad would count Jerome as their educational inspiration.

Perhaps it was because he came from a very poor area of the country himself, perhaps it was the experience of poverty in the West Indies. Whatever the exact reason Jerome arrived at 'Pres' – that bastion of the privileged – with a burning mission for social change. He encouraged a scholarship system which broadened the base of the school-going population. Boys whose families could not keep up with the fees were quietly taken care of. We began to hear of concepts such as social justice, economic fairness.

But his greatest achievement was to set up a house-building programme for the city's elderly poor. In those days Cork suffered a big housing backlog. The tenements were filled with old people living in atrocious poverty. It was a world of dirt and smells and damp. The government paid lip service to the problem but did little about it. The city's rich simply looked the other way. Jerome Kelly changed that.

He set up a group called Share, made up of schoolboys who every week went out to visit the tenements. Then Jerome got us out on the streets with collection boxes. Every Christmas week we would fast and collect. Over the years, the boys of 'Pres' collected millions. Jerome then went to the local authorities and cajoled and persuaded them into putting up money for new houses. Today the city has numerous modern developments that sprang out of Jerome's energy and idealism.

I last saw him in August when he came to lunch at my cottage on a beautiful summer's day. He told me he was fighting leukaemia but was confident of surviving. Most of his talk was about Share and how the housing projects were going from strength to strength. We had become firm friends after I left school, and he would often ring for a chat, wherever I was in the world.

He was a man who made you believe in yourself, even when the evidence suggested you shouldn't. The big idea at the heart of his life was that education was truly more than exam results: it was about the open eye, the open mind, the open heart. He got the academic results, of course, but he made sure we saw the bigger picture.

I travelled from London last Monday when I heard he was seriously ill. I arrived at the hospital thirty minutes after he died. I had been late for him all my life. At school I endlessly straggled in late to be met by his admonishing gaze, and the words: 'Make the effort, boy, make the effort.' I imagined I heard them again this week in a hospital corridor.

ON SPRING STREET

New York, November 1998

New York is a city which means different things to different people. For the author, it's a place which brings back memories of a much-loved relative who died there in 1972.

It is wet and windy in New York. The rain is of the kind that makes taxis disappear and brings the African umbrella salesmen to the doors of the Algonquin Hotel. The rain sweeping in from Long Island drenched the Macy's Thanksgiving Day parade as it passed slowly down Manhattan. All those floats and clowns and football stars soaked by the autumn storm while the television announcers strained to sound cheerful.

I didn't go to the parade, but I saw the highlights on TV and I saw the sodden families in the hotel lobby. Looking at them, I felt tempted to hide indoors for the day, channel-hopping and reading, enjoying the rare pleasure of doing nothing much in a country that had come to a stop. But I had something to do, an appointment with memory down in the small streets near Little Italy.

Whenever I come to New York, I make a point of walking along Spring Street and stopping near the small park, near the intersection with Broadway, where I mumble a prayer to myself before wandering on through Little Italy and Chinatown and back up to midtown, my ritual complete.

I first walked Spring Street in 1980, eight years after Michael had died there in a late-night fire in his apartment. Michael Hassett. Uncle Michael. Mike. Our lost and laughing boy. My grandmother's favourite. The boy who would never be coming home.

The last photograph taken before his death shows a dark-haired, handsome young man smiling at the camera. He is thirty years old and a respected theatre director. America has been good to him. A graduate of Columbia University, he has begun to make a bit of a name for himself off Broadway. He loves the bohemian world of early-seventies Greenwich Village. A world of actors, playwrights, musicians and a great many talkers and dreamers.

He had come to the United States in the late fifties, sailing out of Cobh Harbour like hundreds of thousands of Irish before him. But he was not fleeing poverty or persecution. Michael was the child of a relatively well-to-do middle-class Cork family. He could have stayed at home and found a job. No, Michael left because he was a romantic, a young man whose eyes had, from an early age, been fixed on a world beyond the little streets of Cork city.

When he came to New York, he found a job with General Electric and studied by night. The photographs of those years show a boyish, earnest face. His letters to my grandmother told, in matter-of-fact detail, how he was succeeding at work and college. They told about the people from every corner of the world he was meeting, about his growing interest in the theatre scene, and his ambition to become a director.

And then they began to tell of his relationship with a young woman called Janet and his plans to marry. The marriage went ahead but soon enough ran into trouble. They were children of vastly different worlds and families and, in the end, they divorced.

I do not know the details but I do remember meeting Janet at his funeral in Cork. She was a slight, dark-haired woman and I bored her senseless with endless questions about America.

My own memories of Michael are few. When I see him in my mind's eye, he is wearing a plaid shirt and blue denims and he is laughing. Always laughing. He came home on a visit once when I was about nine or ten. It was August and we were holidaying on the south-east coast, in the village where my grandfather was born.

Michael took me to the beach at Goat Island. I remember him hurling me into the waves. He meant it as a joke but I was terrified and howled miserably. I will never forget his solicitude and tenderness, running into the water to gather me into his arms and hugging me until my crying subsided. I remember, too, a night in Dublin when he came to visit us at the very end of that holiday. He had told my grandmother that he would be coming home for good the following year. There was a job at a theatre in Dublin and he was anxious to take it up. He had had enough of New York. There were some drinks and songs. Michael sang 'Red River Valley' in his rich, melodic voice: 'Come and sit by my side if you love me, do not hasten to bid me adieu.'

That night, we dropped him at the train station and I remember that the train was full of football supporters, returning to Cork after some big game. I felt worried for my uncle. The crowd was noisy and boisterous. I should not have worried. My last image of him is of the smiling face pressed against the window and his hand waving frantically as the train pulled away.

A few months later, on a January night, I was sitting in my grandmother's front room when my uncle Barry arrived. To this day I can remember his exact words. 'I have some bad news for ye,' he said. Bad news.

Michael was dead. There had been a fire in his apartment and he had died trying to escape. I remember muffled cries from another room. The sound of a world collapsing. I knew that the voice was my grandmother's. Later, a doctor came with some injections and pills, and I heard the word 'sedate' for the first time.

There was a funeral with the shiny steel coffin in which Michael's remains had been flown from America. I watched it all from behind the backs of the adults. Children are kept on the edge of such events. They are ushered quickly in and out of them. But they see more than the grown-ups know.

I could tell that my grandmother, a great anchor of my life, had been changed utterly by the loss of her son. I was living with her at the time, my parents having separated a few months before, and so I saw her pain every day. She struggled on with what I can now see was remarkable courage. With young children to look after, she pushed her own feelings into the background and made our lives as happy and secure as she could. But when she spoke of Michael, her eyes filled with tears. This laughing, loving, great woman would never be the same again.

One night, many years later, I was staying in my grandmother's house after going to a dance in the city. When I arrived home, well after midnight, I found my gran sitting up with Michael's photograph in her hands. I made some tea and sat with her. 'Do you think there is a heaven, Ferg?' she asked. 'Do you think I'll see him again, that we'll be together again?'

I spoke for a long time. They were reassuring words, words of belief that I was not very sure of myself but which the old woman needed so badly to hear. I don't know that she believed either. She told me that her own gift for hope had vanished on the night Michael died. And then she said something that I would never, could never, forget. 'Always remember him. Even when you are much older, remember him. And if you have children, tell them about him. Because he was special.'

And that is why, on a rainy Thanksgiving Day, 1998, I walked down Spring Street and whispered a prayer for Michael.

BULLIES

They are the scourge of the playground. The bullies who bring misery to their victims and a guilty pain to their parents. But it isn't just children who suffer. There are bullies at work and in the boardroom too. And like their childish counterparts, they attack the weak because that's the way they have learned to behave.

It is every parent's most cherished illusion and it never survives contact with the world beyond our homes: the belief that somehow we can protect our children from those who would do them harm. I cannot understand why I clung to that belief for so long. After all, I had seen enough of the harm done to children in the world, ample evidence of murder and torture and rape and abandonment. But until this week, I suspect, I had been rather lucky in my own life. Not that I have any great crime or drama to report, just an ordinary story of boys in a playground that ended with a little blood and a lot of tears.

I had taken my son out to play on one of those beautiful late spring evenings earlier this week. It's a small playground, and we know most of the neighbourhood children. The mums and dads stand around and chat while their offspring tumble and swing and slide. Occasionally there is a howl of pain as some child falls from a climbing frame or trips while chasing a football: minor accidents soon cured with soft words. There has never been – when I've been there, at least – any sign of violence. Until this week.

The only other kid in the playground was being looked after by his teenage sister. He was about three years old, the same age as my son. At first he and my son seemed to be playing together happily. Hide and seek, running and chasing.

And then, as they were running towards the swings, the other boy turned around, grabbed my son and wrestled him to the ground. He then started to batter his face with one hand while holding his head down on the ground with the other. This was not playground rough and tumble. There was something vicious in the kid's expression as he set about my son. I was shocked but responded immediately, acting upon some primal urge I suppose, grabbing the youngster and hauling him off.

I screamed something at him, I can't quite remember what. Words of rage that stunned him. The boy's teenage sister arrived and pulled him away. My three-year-old lay on the ground with his lip bleeding and a bump swelling up on his face.

He was – as you might imagine – crying hysterically. My son had never witnessed real-life violence. There is no slapping in our house, and we do our best to filter out the worst excesses of children's television. However, here was my child shaking in my arms, bewildered at the sudden and unprovoked violence that had descended on him. When he did speak, later at home after the application of Savlon and a slice of cake, it was only to say: 'Thanks for rescuing me, Dad.' But I did not feel that I had rescued him. Quite the opposite, in fact. I had failed to protect him from that first, inevitable encounter with aggressive violence.

Later he asked me why the other child had attacked him. There was a lot I could have said but, remembering that he was three years old and pre-rational, I just opted for the 'he's silly and he didn't really mean it' line. It did the trick, but my son would not go to sleep until very late that night. And when he woke up he wondered again about why he had been attacked. What would I have said to him if he had been older? Would I tell him that the world is a frightening place at times and that there are people who will do you harm given half a chance? Or might I instead tell him to become tough and to prepare to meet the challengers who will rise up in playgrounds, schoolyards, playing fields and boardrooms for the rest of his life?

I don't know the true answer to my boy's question. But I suspect the little bully's behaviour was an imitation of some adult in his life. I remember my own first serious encounter with a bully. I was ten years old and had just started at a new school. It was in a strange city and I had a strange accent. I also bore the stigma of having come from a fee-paying institution to this state-funded school. And so, on my first day, a big oaf named Larkin decided to test my mettle.

Larkin came from the country and had fists the size of hams. I remember that his hair always stood on end in the morning and that he was always the first in the queue for the free soup and brown bread that the headmaster doled out at lunch time. Beyond a certain low cunning he seemed a fairly dim character, destined for a life of toil on some unforgiving piece of ground in the west of Ireland.

On that first morning I had just taken my place in the class when Larkin turned around and asked if I was 'handy'. I didn't know it at the time, but 'handy' meant a useful fighter. Assuming that he was being friendly I answered that I was indeed 'handy'. What a mistake. It didn't take long for Larkin and his pals to realize I was anything but 'handy'. I didn't run away from the fights but I never won. It got painful, fighting losing battles, and so I developed an alternative strategy: use cunning to stay one step ahead of them, duck and dive and stay out of their way, use your intelligence to flatter the fools or your wit to put them down. And never cry. If you cried the hyena instinct was awakened, and the bastards would never let you alone.

There were two really, really bad bastards. Boys you avoided like the plague. They had a look in their eyes that said: 'I am capable of anything, just try me.' One day they filled a plastic bag full of piss – several boys were forced to contribute – and poured it over the head of a quiet, sensitive boy who had refused to steal cigarettes for them. They then beat him up for good measure.

The quiet kid went home and, unusually for those days, told his mother. The following day she arrived at the school, marched into the class and pointed out the two villains to the headmaster. They were dragged out and thrashed in front of the woman. It was a savage beating and there were tears and cries. Afterwards the two were expelled from the school.

I always felt I was going to be sick when I watched people being beaten up or being beaten by the headmaster. It was two sides of the same coin: the stronger beating the daylights out of the weaker.

There were a lot of kids in that school who had no defence: neither the physical strength nor the mental cunning to defeat the bullies. And boy, they suffered. They were kids who never offered anybody a minute's harm in their lives. Maybe they stuttered or wore strange clothes or looked funny in some way; maybe they had National Health glasses or buck teeth. Most groups of children have their way of identifying victims – the hyena instinct again. However, the bullies made the leap between recognition of a victim to persecution.

And why? The same why that made a kid attack my son in the playground. It is painfully simple: the strong will turn on the weak if that is the lesson they learn at home or at school. The culture of physical violence is leaving our schools, but it thrives in too many homes. Too many parents believe that to strike and hit is healthy. What madness. Big people hit little people. Those little people hit other weaker people. And so it goes on.

I cannot prove that the boy who attacked my son (a) witnessed violence in his home or (b) was subjected to violence by somebody older. But I would bet that one of the two is a very strong possibility. Children are not born brutal or violent. They are turned into these things by what they see and experience. It is as true in London as it is in Kosovo or in the corridors of Columbine High. What a pity the adults are not learning the lesson.

BY NEWPORT STATION WE
SAT DOWN AND WAITED

Hay-on-Wye, May 1998

**What a shock to realize that the family had travelled the long, slow
route up to the literary festival in Herefordshire only to discover
that the organizers had been laying on chauffeur-driven cars, even
a helicopter, for their other guests. And would young Daniel, who
was accompanying his parents, be all smiles and sweetness, or
would he greet the literati in altogether darker mood?**

By Newport station we sat down and gritted our teeth. Midday
had come and gone with no sign of the train. My two-year-old
son was threatening to jump on to the tracks in search of Thomas
the Tank Engine, my wife was convinced (after years of bitter
experience) that I had misunderstood the timetable and I was
starting to break into a cold sweat.

We were bound for a literary festival at which I was due to read
and answer questions. I pictured a marquee full of patient, earnest
faces awaiting my arrival; waiting and waiting until patience gave
way to rage.

Urged on by my wife, I approached a pale youth wearing the
uniform of the railway company. 'Do you know how late it's
going to be?' I asked. 'I am supposed to be giving a reading at the
Hay Festival in a couple of hours.'

The youth shook his head and simply said: 'What?' Again I
questioned: 'The train. Even a rough idea how late?' He looked at
me with what I took to be pity and replied: 'Ah no. I wouldn't
like to say, sir.' I tried several of his colleagues with an equal lack
of success. Then a woman sitting nearby said she was also on her
way to Hay. 'You'll make it all right. Don't worry,' she said.

As it happened I had returned just the previous day from a

three-week trip to Japan filming for the television series *Great Railway Journeys*. In three weeks, and across countless miles of track, not one train had been late. Steam trains, commuter trains, bullet trains. All had arrived and departed exactly as scheduled. And on the one occasion when a train threatened to be late, the apology was profuse. In this matter at least the Japanese know how to say sorry. When our train rumbled into Newport twenty-five minutes late, was there a word of apology? Of course not.

By the time we neared Hay-on-Wye, the family stress level was heading for the danger zone. But much, much worse was to come. For, as we began the last stage of the journey from Hereford to Hay by car, our charming driver Nigel volunteered a terrible secret: 'We had that John Humphrys from the *Today* programme earlier,' he chirped. 'They sent a helicopter up to London to get him.' A helicopter! From London! While I, the inestimably great Keane was travelling by rail (second class). I was just recovering from the shock of that disclosure when Nigel explained that several other writers not quite in the helicopter class – like Peter Carey – had been chauffeured down from London.

So it was, somewhere between Hereford and Hay-on-Wye, amid the green folds of the summer countryside, that I came face to face with a reality I have evaded for too long: I am not an A-list literary celeb, not even a B-list one. At the very best I am C-list. Perhaps even that is pushing it. If I were a soccer team, I would be lucky to be in the Third Division. If I were a country, I would be Albania or Guinea Bissau.

I was, however, naturally concerned to hear that the arrival of Mr Humphrys' helicopter had terrified a number of cows. They had been innocently munching grass when the whirlybird descended into their field. The creatures must indeed have suffered shock. One can only hope that the trauma was alleviated by the knowledge that a real somebody from the A-list had arrived in their midst.

If, like me, you have produced a book inspired by the arrival of your firstborn, it might seem perfectly natural, even desirable, to bring the said child to an occasional literary event. At the very least, one would be preparing him for a life on the giddy fringes of celebrity. After Hay, it is something I would strongly caution against.

For it is a scientific certainty that the child will become more waspish, fractious and cross the greater the number of adoring readers who surround him. 'Is this the famous Daniel?' they asked and he frowned in return. And woe betide the one who extended a hand to pat his head. This could produce howls of terror.

At Hay, we went to a charming restaurant on the main street for our evening meal. A woman sat alone by the window. To her right was an open book, to her left a glass of white wine. She was contemplating the rooftops and the last beams of sunlight flooding the street. As we approached, she looked up and smiled. 'That little boy looks like one of Botticelli's cherubs, a real sweetie,' she gushed. Ten minutes later, as our cherub loudly demanded a football and stamped his feet on the ground, I saw her shoulder muscles tense, a distinct red flush appearing on her cheeks. The poor woman was struggling. At the best of times, it is impossible to control the moods of a two-year-old. Generations of parents have suffered public humiliation at the hands of such infants.

But where other parents at a literary festival might deliver a stern reprimand, I must observe a public sweetness that demands immense powers of self-control. No barking, no raised voice. 'Now, love, won't you be a good boy?' I whimper. If things are looking desperate I might say: 'If you're not good, the man will be cross.' Just who the man might be is never specified, but his looming presence generally tends to have a quietening effect. And thus, as I ushered the fractious child out of the restaurant and into the street, I imagined the other diners saying: 'Such a nice man, just like in the book.'

The reading itself was a dream: full of ordinary people listening carefully and asking intelligent questions. I always come away from such events feeling slightly guilty. People are, generally speaking, terribly nice. The media swamp I crawl from is so shallow, self-regarding and venal. I love Hunter S. Thompson's description: 'It is a shallow money trench, a long plastic hallway where pimps and thieves run wild and good men die like dogs.' There is, however, the occasional hazard of the lurking crank. I once almost abandoned a reading in Ireland when a supporter of the Angolan government launched a long and bitter tirade against imperialism and its proverbial running dogs. He included me among the galloping canines.

Still worse are the religious fanatics. Believe me, they are out there. Waiting for their moment. You never know the hour when you will look up from a table full of unsold books to find a beatific smile and an invitation to welcome Jesus into your life. Hay-on-Wye was blissfully free of such miseries.

After the reading, I collected Daniel from the patient arms of his mother and headed off across the fields. The sun was shining and my son was in his 'I am the sweetest child in the world' mood. After a few minutes' walking, we came to a field full of sheep. The ground was covered with their tiny black droppings.

'Don't walk on the poo,' I warned. 'Don't walk on the poo,' repeated Daniel. Then he fixed the sheep with a determined stare. 'Let's chase them,' he shouted and galloped off across the poo-pebbled grass, scattering the flocks before him.

WHAT WE TALK ABOUT WHEN WE TALK ABOUT CARVER

Dublin, August 1998

Raymond Carver is not one of those authors whose work is enjoyed but then put aside. His words provide comfort as well as lasting inspiration.

After this week of Clinton and Lewinsky, cabinet reshuffles, child murder and so much other grim news I want to forget everything grey and heavy and spend this Saturday morning thinking of a dead hero, a man whose words have always called me back to the world of the sane. I once read that having a hero diminishes the self. Maybe so. But in the case of Raymond Carver I feel I owe a profound personal debt, one he was never aware of but which obliges me to do him honour on this the tenth anniversary of his death.

Poet, short-story writer and essayist, Raymond Carver became one of the towering figures of contemporary American literature. I only came to him late in my reading life; long after I had devoured Fitzgerald, Faulkner, Hemingway and Bellow. I liked them and admired their craft but I grew to love Carver and in the course of one long dark winter he turned out to be the best friend this boy ever had. But first, for those who know little of the man, a few details.

Raymond Carver was born into a blue-collar family in Oregon in 1935. His father worked in the saw mills, his mother was a waitress and a clerk. They had come up from Arkansas to escape the Great Depression, restless people chasing the moment that would transform their marginal circumstances. But in Carver's childhood world the big dreams withered fast, reduced relentlessly to the small victories of survival. People wanted better for themselves and their children but, as Carver later wrote, their 'luck had gone south'.

The vast world of blue-collar America with its dreary small towns and trailer parks would later become the primary landscape of his fiction and poetry, a world that no writer before has evoked with such honesty and power. Consider these few lines from the poem 'Photograph of My Father in His Twenty-second Year'.

> But the eyes give him away,
> and the hands
> that limply offer the string of
> dead perch and
> the bottle of beer. Father I love
> you, yet how
> can I say thank you, I who
> can't hold my
> liquor either, and don't even
> know the places
> to fish?

Carver married young and worked at a succession of low-paid jobs. With two children to support, his writing took second place to the imperatives of family life. Like his father before him he was gradually beaten down by alcoholism. The drinking wrought havoc in his own life and in the lives of those he loved. Some of the finest writing anywhere on the subject of that lonely disease is to be found in Carver's short fiction and poems – the world of black depressions and shaking hands, drying-out clinics, broken promises, betrayals, sick stomachs and shame. You have to live there to know it; Carver did and he described it with searing honesty.

I came to Carver through my father. Some months before his death from the effects of alcoholism he sent me a copy of Carver's collected stories. The book was, I think, a quiet message. Read this, it seemed to say, and you will know what it is like to live in my world and with that knowledge you will never see things in quite the same way again. I read the book and felt as if I had been hit by a thunderbolt, the jolt of recognition both liberating and painful. That weekend I went out and bought everything of Carver's I could find. It was the poetry which most directly addressed the alcoholic world.

> It was then that I remembered
> back to those days
> and how telephones used to
> jump when they rang.
> And the people who would come
> in those early-morning
> hours to pound on the door in
> alarm. Never mind the
> alarm felt inside.
> I remembered that, and gravy
> dinners. Knives lying
> around, waiting for trouble.
> Going to bed and hoping
> I wouldn't wake up.
> ('The Old Days')

This is writing stripped of pretence. Direct but not bludgeoning, artful but never arch. The language is ordinary but not in a self-conscious or patronizing way. A poet who had to imagine that marginal world, who had not lived it, could all too easily sound condescending or resort to dramatics. Carver understood that the true agony of that world was its dreariness and shame. There were sudden explosions, yes, but the real damage was in the endlessness, the slow choking-off of possibility, the aching silences that followed each binge and hospitalization. With Carver you read it as it really was.

In 1976, after several hospitalizations brought about by his drinking, Carver finally quit alcohol. In the same period his first marriage collapsed and he met the writer Tess Gallagher, with whom he was to spend the last eleven years of his life. Along with that happy relationship, and his growing literary fame and financial security, came a sense of inner peace. It wasn't that Carver had forgotten the world he had just left – far from it. But he had found the strength to deal with his ghosts.

His final collection, *A New Path to the Waterfall*, was written as he battled with the cancer that would invade first his lungs and then his brain. It is a remarkable work both for its absence of self-pity and Carver's celebration of the life that was slowly ebbing away from him.

As the cancer attacked, Carver and Tess Gallagher worked against the clock to complete the book. The result, in poems like 'Hummingbird', is an extraordinary tenderness, simplicity and directness:

> *Suppose I say summer,*
> *write the word 'hummingbird',*
> *put it in an envelope, take it*
> *down the hill to the box.*
> *When you open my letter you*
> *will recall those days and how*
> *much, just how much I love you.*

I lived with that book by my side in the months around my father's death; I cannot remember how many times it rescued me from the depths. In the way that some men cling to prayer books I clasped *New Path to the Waterfall*. But for me Carver's writing was about more than simple empathy. To borrow Fitzgerald's lines about Gatsby, it was Carver's 'extraordinary gift for hope' that saw me through.

No matter where or who you've been, he seemed to say, there

is another, sweeter life to be had. It is a life you have to work for but a life that is your right. They were the words of a dying man but to read into them some kind of last-minute 'religious' awakening would be mistaken. Carver would never have fallen for anything so glib.

The good news is that Carver's collected poems have been published in a single volume, entitled *All of Us*. To those who haven't yet discovered him, I cannot recommend this book highly enough. You don't have to be the child of an alcoholic home to find resonance in Carver's work. It is ultimately a meditation on the things which shape all of our lives: loneliness, fear, hope, loss, love. More than anything love. I leave you with the last and shortest poem in the book, 'Late Fragment'. Carver wrote it in the final stages of his illness. It is my favourite.

> And did you get what
> you wanted from this life, even so?
> I did.
> And what did you want?
> To call myself beloved, to
> feel myself
> Beloved on the earth.

LEAVING HOME

Santiago, October 1998

Setting off on an assignment overseas can be an emotional business. There are the rituals of departure: the bag packed at dawn, the sleepy farewells, the taxi to the airport. And then, a chance to meet up with the colleagues who'll be constant companions during the days and weeks which lie ahead.

It really begins to kick in during the last three days. It may be a trip you have known about for weeks but because thinking about it involves all kinds of unpleasant possibilities, you tend to push reality away. And then the exigencies of travel make further evasion impossible. The phone calls from the office multiply. Queries about air tickets, money and tips, and advice from others who have travelled the route before you. There are crackly phone calls from fixers with exotic names in far-away places promising to meet you at the airport or haggling over their daily rate. It could be an Amir in Afghanistan, Kumi in Colombo, Victor in Johannesburg, or a hundred other names familiar to the people of the road.

I love travel but I hate the leaving; the sense of instability and insecurity it creates in the atmosphere. That is why I try to pack my bag when there is nobody else in the house, always at the last minute. And once packed I try to hide it away. Who am I fooling? Of course my loved ones know I am going but somehow I feel that bag sitting in the hallway is too empty a sight for all of us.

There was a time when I derided those of my colleagues who were superstitious. Martin Bell's white suit was not for me. Too theatrical by half, I thought. But something has been happening because these days I too carry charms. There is a Khmer scarf I picked up in Cambodia; a small wooden icon of the Madonna and Child; and my beloved Claddagh ring. The Claddagh is a gold ring with two hands intertwined around a heart and above them a crown. Love, honour and friendship is the general idea. I never travel without it.

Why the superstition after all those years of sneering disbelief? I think it has something to do with age. I am lurching towards the big forty and I am looking forward to my seventieth birthday. Anything I can possibly do to ward off bad luck, I will do. When I am heading off to one of the world's bad lands, I do my best to avoid thinking about the possible dangers. I assess the risks as best as possible, and with that done, I try to push the darker thoughts to one side.

When colleagues of your own generation have died in war zones, there is naturally a much greater awareness of mortality. Suddenly death is no longer only something that happens to the people you are reporting on: the high-velocity round, the shell fragment, the machete blow – they all smash through the illusion of invulnerability. Brief yourself well but do not dwell on the fearful possibilities. That way madness lies.

I like to leave early in the morning when everybody is asleep. No time then for sad goodbyes. I move around the silent house gathering my bits and pieces, gulp down a black coffee and wait for the growl of the taxi in the street outside. But on this latest trip to Africa it didn't quite work out like that. I was shaving in the bathroom when I heard a knock on the door. I opened it and saw my three-year-old son standing there sleepy-eyed. 'My name is Daniel Patrick Alexander,' he said, as if answering a question put by an invisible stranger. The poor child was half asleep. Something had woken him. A dream perhaps, or was it my presence moving around the house?

I picked him up and he fell asleep again within seconds. Feeling him close to me, sleepy and warm, I wanted to pick up the telephone and cancel the trip. But I couldn't and so I carried him to our bedroom and settled him in beside his mother. And then I crept out and down the stairs on to the street. I needed the car to come; I needed to be moving; I needed to get a grip on my emotion.

And so I left for another early morning rendezvous at the airport. Oh Heathrow, oh Heathrow – that forlorn temple of the foreign correspondent. The sight of my travelling colleagues Kevin and Nigel greatly cheered me up. In this business you choose your fellow travellers with as much care as possible. If you are going to dangerous or unstable places, you need people who don't panic, who are not gung-ho merchants, and who have a strong sense of humour. Kevin and Nigel are two such gents, specialists in the black humour of the road.

There is one vital ritual to complete before leaving Heathrow: the purchase of whiskey and cigarettes. These are not for our own consumption – honestly – but our gifts for potentially useful and co-operative people at the other end. Believe me, many an army colonel has been charmed by the introduction of a bottle of Johnny Walker into the conversation. The cigarette has been the passport to co-operation at many a dodgy road block: first the handshake (never let go of a man's hand in such a situation – he is much less likely to blow you away if he can feel your hand in his) and then the offer of a smoke. For the really unco-operative road block, I offer a packet of cigarettes; for the psychotic, a whole carton. The whiskey, of course, must never ever be produced at a road block. The men blocking your way may already be drunk. The last thing they need is firewater that will rev them up even more.

The road can be a very lonely place. Where there are telephones it is possible to mitigate the loneliness. Nothing is sweeter than the voice of a loved one over the distant miles. You long to hear the most banal of domestic detail. What is the latest on the tiling job in the kitchen? Has the boy's cold gone yet? After what can sometimes be days of horror and fear, you live for the soft, reassuring voice of the normal. At night, when the beers come out and we are all congregated in someone's hotel room (it is the luckless Kevin's, the youngest of us on this trip), we start out with stories of other places we have been.

There is almost an element of besting one another: 'You think that was bad. Wait until I tell you about Kisangani.' But sooner or later we end up talking about home and those we miss. Kevin is talking about football a lot on this trip, but then he always does. He is a Queens Park Rangers fan, a devoted one despite some cruel mockery from the rest of us. Kevin's great strength is his calm. I have yet to see him lose his temper, which, when travelling in Africa, is some testament to his forbearance. Big Nigel is a prince of the road: the man who for several years in Bosnia was cameraman to Martin Bell. You feel safe around big Nigel. He has a lucky aura.

We have a lot of work to do here. Long days among some very strange people. But home is just a week away. And on the road that is what you live for: homecoming. It is that indescribable feeling when the taxi slows to a halt outside your front door and your child's face appears at the window, laughing. And then you promise yourself you will not go to such places again. And this time you really do mean it.

Part Two

FROM A
EUROPEAN WAR

THE GRAVE

Sarajevo, March, 1999

The horrors of the Balkan war continued to be unearthed long after the conflict was brought to an end in 1995. The city of Sarajevo, scene of some of the most bitter fighting, has been rebuilt; but there's still evidence on all sides of the struggle and the suffering of its residents.

Riyalda met me at Sarajevo airport. She was nervous and shy and smoked one cigarette after another. She asked me if I had been to Sarajevo before. I replied that it was my first time in the Balkans. 'Well, you've got quite an education in front of you,' she said. We drove along Snipers Alley and there were traffic cops giving out speeding tickets. 'Normality,' said Riyalda and she laughed. I had nothing to compare this scene to. I had no past here. Many of my friends had covered this war, some had lost their hearts to the place. But to me it was a city glimpsed only occasionally on the evening news. I watched the Bosnian war from a long way off. In those days I was living in South Africa and much too caught up in what was happening there to learn very much about Sarajevo or Srebrenica. What I knew of the Balkans was gleaned from BBC World Service radio and the snippets of news carried by South African television.

My first thought was how ugly it all looked. In the dark I could see only blocks of modern housing and some burned-out buildings. Riyalda lived in an apartment in one of those blocks. Her father had been a soldier in the Yugoslav army – a Muslim – and her mother was a Serb. Riyalda had grown up in Belgrade and only moved to Sarajevo as a teenager when her father was transferred by the military. He died a year before the war broke out and Riyalda thanks heaven for that. Her mother is not well and stays inside the flat most of the time. I wanted to ask what it is like for a Serb woman to live surrounded by Muslims but I didn't know Riyalda well enough to tread on such delicate ground.

We drove to the Holiday Inn and saw a group of teenagers playing around a fountain. Riyalda said that in the war days they would have been killed by snipers in a few seconds. In the war days nobody would have dreamed of standing out in the open like that. That night she took us to a restaurant a few minutes' walk away. In the window beside my head there was a bullet hole. The waiter explained that it had been there since the war; they left it as a little reminder of what the city had gone through.

That night, around the corner from the Holiday Inn, I found a bar run by an Irishman which stayed open late and served Guinness. He had come over to work with the international police force in Bosnia and when the contract finished decided to stay on. He loved the place, he said, and he was making a good living. The bar was full of UN workers and there were some Irish army officers. I made the mistake of drinking too much and got into an argument with one of my fellow countrymen. He was of the opinion that every side in Bosnia was as bad as the other. It was wrong to blame Milosevic for all of this, he said. Tudjman and Izetbegovic were just as much at fault. A blanket of blame was dropped equally on all of their heads.

I resented this man. There was something too smug about his attitude. It was the same rubbish I'd heard in Rwanda: they've been at it for years and they always will be. It's inevitable. They hate each other. Blame them all and you don't have to worry about taking any responsibility for what happens. The argument became heated and I tried to score stupid points. Had he ever heard a shot fired in anger? Had he ever been in war? Did he ever see what happens when politicians set one group of people on another? And he said no he had never been in war and had never seen ethnic hatred erupting into violence. Somewhere in the back of my drunken brain I could hear what my voice really sounded like.

Sanctimonious, hectoring, declamatory. And so I shut up and finished my drink and went home.

The following morning we drove to Tuzla. The US marines had found a mass grave at a place called Donja Glumina between Tuzla and Zvornik. A team of forensic experts had helped unearth the bodies – there were 130 in all – and they were to be displayed in Tuzla so that relatives might make an identification. It was a bright spring morning and driving through the countryside I remarked to Riyalda that it reminded me of home. Green fields, woodland, cattle in the fields. 'Like Ireland,' she said, 'but about a hundred times more crazy.' All along the way we passed abandoned houses, the homes of the ethnically cleansed. At several points along the road we saw long ribbons of yellow tape and signs that warned of mines. Riyalda talked non-stop as we drove.

In Tuzla we went straight to the mortuary where the bodies were being prepared for identification. I recognized the smell from a long way off. The moment we got out of the car outside the morgue it swamped us – high, bitter, nauseating. You could stand near it for a few minutes but no more. The doctor in charge introduced himself as Stefan. He and his colleagues wore green surgical gowns and rubber gloves but they had no face masks. 'After a while you get so used to the smell you ignore it,' said Dr Stefan.

We followed him into a courtyard where there were mounds of filthy plastic bags, each the length of an average human being. The bags had been flattened out and were covered with mud. A worker came with a hose and began to spray them. The mud spattered in all directions and I jumped out of the way. As he cleaned, so did the contents of the bags become more visible. A boot peeked out here, a skeletal hand there. There were serial numbers on most of the bags.

Dr Stefan explained that they were Yugoslav army bags. For the record the bodies we were about to see were those of the men of Donja Glumina, a village outside Zvornik, one of the first towns to be 'cleansed' at the beginning of the war. Zvornik was where Arkan and his Tigers were given free rein by the army to slaughter Muslims. The corpses here were about six years old but Dr Stefan said identification would still be possible in quite a few cases. The doctors worked patiently through the afternoon, cutting away at bags so that the cleaners could wash away much of the mud and ooze which had gathered around the bodies.

Inside the mortuary another group of cleaners was washing clothes. Scraps, really, more than full items of clothing. The hose swished on and on across trousers and sweaters and jackets. Maybe a relative would come and recognize a particular shirt or jacket, whatever it was her husband or brother or son was wearing when the Serbs hauled him away. In the late afternoon the cleaners paused. A boy came out from the town with a large bag of kebabs and a crate of beer. And there in the stink and mulch of death the men sat down to eat their dinner. Like Dr Stefan said, it was something you got used to, working around here.

The following morning I went down to the mortuary just after eight o'clock. Relatives had already started to gather on the road outside. It was misty and very cold and many of the people waiting were shivering. I heard a woman remark on the smell. But the woman beside her didn't respond. Dr Stefan was there supervising the cleaners as they laid out one body after another in a long rectangle. It was the first time I had seen the actual bodies as distinct from the muddy bags. A piece of white paper with a number scrawled on it had been placed on each corpse. And beside them, too, were any items that had been found in the pockets. Things which had not rotted away in the intervening six years. There were watches, spectacles, an insulin needle. There were pens and wallets and some prayer beads. The corpses were badly decomposed. But I could tell from many of the faces that these men had died in agony. Again and again I saw mouths cast wide open in expressions of profound agony.

Soon after that the relatives started to come in. The doctors escorted them gently around the line of bodies. Shouts rose up. Cries of anguish. People became hysterical and were led away. Men's names were shouted out. I heard a girl cry, 'Mustapha, Mustapha.' She fell on the ground and medics rushed to help her. Soon they were running here and there dealing with people who had recognized a fragment of some lost loved one. Two women appeared supporting an elderly man. He collapsed onto a chair where doctors tried to help him. I was told that his name was Rifat Osmanovic and he had just found the body of his son. Others walked repeatedly along the line of bodies but could find nothing to recognize. And which was the sadder, I wondered: Rifat Osmanovic and the others who had at last traced their dead children, or the mothers who would leave here with nothing revealed, nothing known.

We left the mortuary and went back to the town. In the skies above us NATO jets were rumbling, reconnaissance and training missions around Kosovo, a conflict that was waiting to explode. In town a group of Bosnian army officers had arrived at the Tuzla hotel. I asked one of them if he thought the country was getting back to normal. He laughed and asked what I meant by 'normal'. I left the conversation at that.

MACEDONIAN SPRING

Skopje, April 1999

The effects of the Kosovo crisis were spreading like ripples on a pond. Neighbouring Macedonia had to cope with an invasion of refugees as well as an army of visiting media and military. And it was making Macedonians feel resentful and frightened.

I was coming out of the Continental Hotel when the sound of the explosion rolled over the mountain. 'Boom boom NATO,' shouted the taxi-driver. The tremor had distracted him from the important question of what fare I should pay. With hundreds of journalists in town, the predatory instincts of Skopje's taxi-men are rampant. All journeys involve a protracted haggle, but my driver had been unnerved by what he imagined were the sounds of war across the border and he wanted to talk politics. 'Clinton bloody crazy. Milosevic bloody crazy. Everybody crazy,' he said. I had to agree. After three days in Macedonia I feel I have entered a narrative of the most profound strangeness. It is three hours from England as the crow flies and, as I write, the same spring sunshine is bathing London and Skopje. But in fifteen years of reporting from war zones I have never felt the same degree of strangeness, the feeling of a world turned upside down.

You start out at the Swissair desk at Heathrow airport, and stand in line behind the people heading for skiing holidays in the Alps. There are bright clothes and there is a lot of laughter. There are many businessmen in the queue. Serious men in fine suits travelling to Geneva and Zurich. One of them is talking on a mobile phone and stops his conversation abruptly as my flak jacket and helmet topple from the trolley and clank on to the floor. But apart from this brief upset, it is a normal morning in Europe.

In Zurich the sun is shining and the Swiss countryside is neat and pretty and safe. And then, more quickly than you can imagine, you are coming in to land at Skopje amid the rows of NATO transport planes. Just outside the window a US marines helicopter, door gunner scanning the ground, is taking off in the direction of the city.

Officially this is a peaceful country that wants a closer relationship with the West, but from the very first conversations it is obvious that the Macedonians would like all of us – journalists, NATO soldiers, aid workers – to go home. My first driver said he was only taking the fare because he needed the money badly. 'You come here and tell lies, nothing but lies. That is what you people are paid to do. You want to make us look like savages,' he said. And then he began to press me for my opinion. What did I think of NATO bombing Yugoslavia? And those Albanians, what did I think of them? I dissembled. I fudged. 'Well of course, I have just arrived in the country. It's so hard to form an instant impression,' I replied. The driver was having none of it. 'You watch TV, you read the newspapers. Of course you have an opinion,' he barked.

I told him that I came from a small country myself and always resented having strangers telling me what was wrong with the place. I could understand his anger at the media and Western politicians. These banal platitudes seemed to satisfy him and he got around to telling me his opinions. We were passing through an Albanian section of town, and the driver did not like the mosques and minarets and the way the women wore scarves and the way the men always seemed to be plotting something under their breath. He had driven a wealthy Albanian family to the Albanian border the other day and they hadn't spoken a word to him all the way. 'They thought they were better than me. The truth, which you foreigners won't tell, is that they want to take this place over. Have you seen how big the families are?' He pointed at a group of children playing soccer in a park. 'They have ten, fifteen children so that they can outnumber us. And now that the refugees have come across, they think they will have a Greater Albania soon.'

By the time we reached the Aleksander Palace hotel, the driver had worked himself into a frenzy of disgust for these Albanians who wanted to drive him out of his own country. It was a familiar diatribe. I had heard it in one form or another in Belfast, Rwanda, South Africa and a few other hotbeds of ethnic conflict. The fear that somebody will take what we have, that somebody will want to change us into something we are not, the fear that they will swamp us and that we will cease to be ourselves. It is the psychology of the threatened and it eats away at fine notions of tolerance and inclusivity. I don't suggest that all Macedonians feel this way about the Albanians, but most of those I've spoken to feel that they are under threat and that NATO's attacks on Slobodan Milosevic are simply pushing them one step closer to a bitter ethnic battle.

And so when you ask yourself how on earth the Macedonian government could have treated the Albanian refugees with such obvious contempt – confining them at the border, forcing them on to buses and planes to get them out of the country – consider the fear and the barely suppressed anger of the majority population here. They have thus far escaped being dragged into the Yugoslavian wars of succession. It has taken a political guile of which few Western politicians would be capable to deal with what correspondents like to call a 'fragile ethnic balance'. In other words, any increase in the resident Albanian population – at present some fifteen per cent of the national total – and you are sliding towards disaster.

It is not hard to understand why the Macedonians would want rid of the refugees as quickly as possible. But the forced expulsions have left a deep reservoir of bitterness. The Kosovo Albanians feel that they have been treated like animals. As Mimoza Butugi, a twenty-one-year-old law student from Pristina, told me: 'They beat us and forced us on to buses. They wouldn't tell us where we were going. I feel as if I am lost in space. I have run out of words for the way I feel. Yes, animals, that is how they made us feel.'

I met her, crammed into a room with twenty other people, in a decrepit Albanian army base in the border town of Pogradec. They had just spent eleven hours on buses, winding over mountain roads as the Macedonians pushed them yet further away from Kosovo. It was an extraordinary sight, central to that narrative of strangeness I spoke about earlier. Here they were: lawyers, doctors, factory workers, farmers, even a music teacher . . . a whole community uprooted and pushed from one country to another country to another country.

The refugees could not care less about a Greater Albania. They simply want to go home. I asked Mimoza if she blamed NATO for her plight. Hadn't the air strikes sparked the ethnic cleansing which drove her and thousands of others from their homes? She did not agree. 'When the air strikes came we ran to the cellar and cheered. You know, we celebrated. And every time we hear on the news that there is an air strike, we cheer again even though we are driven away from our homes. Who was it who drove us from our homes? It was not NATO, not NATO. It was the Serbs who did it.'

We have heard a lot about unclear war aims and bad planning in the past few weeks. I don't know enough about military affairs to talk authoritatively on the question of planning and intelligence. But as for war aims, I am willing to speculate. It may have started out as a war to impose a peace agreement on Milosevic. But it has become something quite different now. It has become a battle for Mimoza and the hundreds of thousands of others who have been driven from their homes at gunpoint and made dependent on the uncertain mercy of strangers; and it is a battle, too, for the memory of those who were cleansed from Zvornik and Srebrenica and a hundred other towns in the long calvary of the former Yugoslavia. It is about saying 'never again' and meaning it.

'EASY' AND THE BOYS

Albania, May 1999

The spring of 1999 saw a crisis in the Balkans. Serbian police and paramilitaries were carrying out a brutal programme of ethnic cleansing in Kosovo. Hundreds of thousands fled their homes and arrived, as refugees, in neighbouring Albania and Macedonia.

> 'Once we had a country and we thought it fair,
> Look in the atlas and you'll find it there:
> We cannot go there now, my dear, we cannot go there now'
> W. H. Auden, 'Ten Songs', March 1939

All week we have watched them. Tractors, lorries, coaches, cars – all crowded with the lost people of Kosovo. We have seen them coming on foot, too, holding what few belongings they managed to save, carrying their children and their old people. It is the saddest procession I have ever seen. There have been times when, standing at the border, I have struggled to believe the evidence of my eyes, when I have asked if the weeping and traumatized people, those ragged and exhausted creatures, really belong in this time and place: Europe, nineteen hundred and ninety-nine.

Not your Europe or my Europe, mind you. Not the Europe of espresso bars and bookshops and museums, but four hours from London all the same. Still part of our continent and still part of our time. One couple and their two little boys came across at the start of the week. The man sat in the driver's seat of the car and was crying. He was ashamed of this and covered his face with a blanket. His wife said she wanted to say something. 'The fires are everywhere. The fires are everywhere,' she said.

The woman was a civil engineer and her husband a teacher. The two boys in the back were looking at their parents weeping.

At first I thought they were embarrassed, and then the younger boy reached forward and put his hand on his father's shoulder. His father, who had hidden his face from us, then leaned over and spoke: 'If you want to help, then help quickly. The people are starving, the people are dying. Help us, help us quickly.' He was speaking not to us, of course, but to NATO. And, having said his few words, the man drove on with his family, following the convoy of the dispossessed to the crowded refugee camps at Kukes, in Albania.

By now there are many of you who feel they have seen and heard and read too much of this misery. A colleague on the phone from London during the week described how she struggled to watch the news these days. She felt overpowered by the terrible images that kept flowing out of Albania. Up here in Kukes there is no off button. There is no other channel to switch to.

Please don't read that as a complaint. I am here because I want to be. I don't know of another story more important or more urgent. But there is no going home at night from this story. The town of Kukes is crammed with refugees and their stories. There is the old man who sits around the yard of the house all day. He keeps to himself and doesn't talk much. He saw his two sons shot dead by the Serbs. There is a family I came across on the street nearby who were standing around crying (you see this so often). And when I asked why, the father explained that he had just returned from Switzerland and, against all odds, had found his wife and three children in the street. 'We are crying with happiness,' he explained.

There are several refugee families sharing our house, and they have become our friends. There is 'Easy', the genial chef from Mitrovica, and his wife and two little children. 'Easy' does the shopping each day and keeps the house in some sort of order. The kids – Medina, aged seven, and her brother Din, four – have become complete pets. In a houseful of war-wearied reporters, cameramen, producers and engineers, they weave a magical spell.

Din found a Hallowe'en mask the other morning and roamed the house 'frightening' everybody. After a night filled with the rumble of NATO jets overhead, it is a kind of blessing to wake and hear their laughing voices.

There is Ilir and his brother Bekem, who were driven with their families from the town of Prizren. Ilir is a jazz pianist, and Bekem ran his own clothing stall in the central market.

And then there is Arber, who this week found his father. I had noticed that everywhere we went he would ask among the crowds if they had heard any news of the men of Gjakova. This same young boy had spent hours translating the refugees' accounts of how the men in the convoys were being abducted. And so Arber was afraid for his father. And then on Wednesday night we pulled up outside the house and Ilir ran out shouting and gesticulating. I did not understand what was said and was only conscious of Arber jumping out of our car and racing across the gravel. Near the door he turned around and shouted: 'My father is here; he is safe.'

That night we met Arber's father. He was exhausted and unshaven but he was alive. We drank his health and he and Arber went off on their own for a celebratory meal. Later in the week we all watched the news reports of Bill Clinton's visit to Germany and listened to his rousing defence of human rights and mutual tolerance.

'Easy' and the rest of the boys were not really convinced. They wonder if Clinton really intends to fight on until victory. They fear a diplomatic fudge that will leave Milosevic in power, and safe to fight another day. They also heard the US President urge them not to be vengeful. They are not, as it happens; they just want to go home. As W. B. Yeats wrote: 'Too long a sacrifice can make a stone of the heart.' Thinking of the Americans' refusal to contemplate fighting Milosevic on the ground, where it matters, I remembered some more lines of Yeats: 'The best lack all conviction, while the worst are full of passionate intensity.'

Mr Milosevic certainly has all the passionate intensity. As for Western conviction, I can only say that the refugees here were much more impressed with Tony Blair's speech in Macedonia than they were with Clinton's in Germany. They believe that Mr Blair will not let them down.

However, it was the statement of another distant politician that really upset 'Easy' and the others. A colleague in London had faxed to us the remarks of Alan Clark, the MP for Kensington and Chelsea, who warned of criminal gangs descending on Britain, hidden among the refugees. He also wondered where the refugee children would be educated (did he fear the corruption of our schools?).

I am not sure how many refugees Mr Clark has met. It could well be that his statement was based on his own solid research rather than on nasty prejudice. Here in Kukes we have no way of knowing.

However, I have met a great many of these refugees. I have interviewed scores of them in Albania and Macedonia. And for two weeks now I have lived with several refugee families. I know that 'Easy' and his family and Ilir, Bekem and Arber are the kind of decent, hard-working people we should be proud to welcome to Britain. They are not liars or cheats or drunks. They most certainly are not criminals. The simple truth is that the overwhelming majority of refugees just want to go home. They don't want to be exiled in Britain or anywhere else. 'Easy' wants us to come and visit him in Kosovo once it has been liberated. 'You will come and I will cook a big meal and we will party all night long.'

And the thing is, I believe it will happen. 'Easy' and his children and all the others living in our house will go home. I do believe that Tony Blair will keep his promise, and that will make it damn near impossible for those with less courage to wriggle out of their responsibility.

KUKES NIGHTS

Rome, May 1999

The Kosovo crisis was deepening. NATO was carrying out air attacks on Serbia. The Chinese embassy in Belgrade was bombed by mistake. The refugees from Kosovo who'd arrived in Albania began to wonder if they would ever return home.

In the dark of the Kukes night it is dangerously easy to miss the open manholes in whose filthy depths swarm armies of fierce rats. On the main street near the Gjalicia hotel there is a hole large enough to swallow a small car. And then there is the three-legged dog – the TV crews call him Tripod – who sleeps in the middle of the road. He has been stepped on four or five times that I've seen, but he still won't quit the square for somewhere safe. Tripod howls when somebody stands on him but never learns the lesson that his sleepy town has changed: there are thousands more trampling feet he must watch out for.

On my last night, I walked from the Bar America to our house by the lake. It was close to midnight and as we crossed the square I noticed that several thousand new refugees had arrived from the border.

The big white tents set up by the World Food Programme were already full to overflowing and so the new arrivals were sleeping in the open. I hate that old cliché 'strangely quiet', but that is exactly what it was.

There were a few rustling sounds here and there as people tossed and turned under their blankets and I heard the occasional cry of a baby. But if I closed my eyes nothing would have suggested that about four thousand people were camped out on the ground in front of me.

Six weeks into the war and they are still flooding across. Sixteen thousand crossed over last weekend. 'Who could be left?' we have asked ourselves. How many more tractors and trailers full of weeping women and children, how many more lines of exhausted ghosts trudging out of the country of the lost? The answer, of course, is that there are many left inside: terrified and hungry, hiding in the forests or waiting for the Serbs to reach their house or their village. I walked on past the sleepers and the Albanian special police and the army lorries and the line of tractors that had formed up alongside our house.

From the road I could see that the lights were still on in the kitchen. 'Easy' – the chef from Mitrovica – was sitting on the couch when I went in, staring out of the window into the blackness. His brother and sister-in-law had come out of Kosovo the day before and there had been a small celebration. 'Easy' was happier than most of us had seen him in weeks.

But tonight the old sadness had come down again. It rolled in on top of him like a coastal fog and he was grasping for a fixed point. All of the things the rest of us hold on to for comfort – our homes, our jobs, our extended families, our physical landscapes – had been taken from him when the Serbs descended on his home town. 'Do you still think we will go home?' he asked.

After the bombing of the Chinese embassy, and with thousands of refugees still arriving in Kukes, 'Easy' was feeling very uncertain. I told him that this had been a dark week, but these were the weeks when leadership mattered, and if people kept their heads and remembered that nothing had happened to alter the justice of the cause then, yes, he and the other refugees would be going home.

But I don't think 'Easy' believed me this time. He shook his head and said that he was tired and then went upstairs to the small room that he shares with Kia and the two children, Medina and Din.

I know that his wife Kia has been feeling the strain more than usual: as the weeks have dragged on and the war has seemed to go nowhere, she has been thinking about what will happen when the winter comes.

Will they still be refugees? Will the journalists with whom they have set up home move on, leaving them alone once more? And what will happen to her two beautiful children upon whom all these foreigners dote? Because sooner or later the excitement of those days – and they are in a strange way, very exciting – will lapse into the numbing tedium of long-term exile.

There is still hope now. But soon enough it will begin to depart. People still believe – not as much as they did at the start, of course – that NATO will triumph before the autumn. But hope is edging away; it is the kind of thing that departs incrementally, until one day the refugees may wake up and find they no longer have a country to call their own.

Kia and 'Easy' are devoted parents. They do everything to protect Medina and Din from the reality of their situation. Every day Kia goes into the square and she can see the ragged and grime-encrusted shadows who queue up to get on coaches for the refugee camps of the south. They are her people but she does not want to join them on that journey into deep exile.

Conditions in our house may be crowded but it is a happy place, and being with foreigners offers some kind of protection. The other day she brought out some special clothes, something she had managed to save when the Serbs ordered them out: a pair of dungarees with a Mickey Mouse logo for Din and a pair of bright orange dungarees for Medina. And then clutching her children's hands tightly, Kia set off across the square, smiling and joking and refusing to be a refugee.

Watching them go, I remembered something 'Easy' said to me when we visited one of the camps last week. 'Refugee, isn't that the saddest word in the world?' he said. We had been watching a group of children reciting poems and making little patriotic speeches at a Unicef counselling session. A seven-year-old girl had stood up and announced that the Kosovars would never live with the Serbs again. 'They think they have driven us out. But we will be back,' she said. Other children followed. All recited speeches and poems in a similar vein; it was depressing stuff. And then they sang some songs of Kosovo and I looked around and saw that tears were streaming down 'Easy''s face. And when he said he loved his country, I could believe that this was real patriotism; not jingoism or sentimentality but a statement of true belonging.

I left Kukes yesterday and I am writing this column in Rome, on a day brimming with the heat of early summer. How strange it is to be here among the great treasures of a lost empire, to walk the ancient streets and to find myself seeking among the crowds the faces of those I have left behind. 'Easy' and Kia and Medina and Din, Arber and Bekem. My friends with no country, I will remember you.

On the way out of Kukes I queued at the helicopter pad next to the Italian refugee camp, waiting for one of the United Nations' choppers that flies between Northern Albania and Tirana. A refugee had come with a desperately sick child. The little girl had contracted some disease and needed to be transferred to hospital abroad. Her father was told that he could not come with her. I don't know why. Bureaucracy, rules, regulations. As the chopper lifted into the sky and the rotors blew dust across on top of us, the man covered his face and wept. And then it was my turn to go. Seventeen-year-old Arber – he is the youngest of our translators – had come to see me off. As the chopper climbed above the camp, I saw Arber giving me a V-for-Victory sign and then as we rose higher I saw the new line of refugee tractors that was coming down from the border in the clear May sunlight.

THE JUDGING OF MILOSEVIC

Athens, April 1999

As NATO stepped up its bombing of Yugoslavia, media organizations in the West were quick to demonize President Milosevic, to compare him with Hitler. Yet, despite the evil deeds carried out in his name in Kosovo, this was neither a fair, nor an accurate, comparison.

They've all been at it these past few weeks. From Washington to London to Belgrade, the ghost of the Austrian corporal has been summoned up and set to work. On Serbian television we have been treated to the spectacle of Blair and Clinton being compared to Hitler; our own media outlets, urged on by official sources, have been quick to compare Milosevic with the great Fascist monster.

The word 'genocide' has also been bandied about a great deal. On the streets of Athens, where I've spent the past few days, the freshly sprayed graffiti feature a NATO symbol upon which a swastika has been superimposed. At political rallies you repeatedly hear the chant of 'Clinton fascisti, Blair fascisti'. This, mind you, in a city that would have had a long-term future in the German Reich had it not been for the efforts of the same Allied forces that now form the backbone of NATO. The Greek Communists delight in comparing Blair and Clinton with the Fascist dictators of the thirties. There is, naturally enough, no comparison made between Milosevic and great Communist monsters such as Stalin.

But these are days when history is being twisted and abused. When the refugees began to pour out of Kosovo a fortnight ago, British newspapers fell over themselves to tell us that this had 'eerie echoes of the Second World War'. What they meant was that the trains carrying people out of Kosovo into forced exile reminded journalists of the grim carriages of Auschwitz and Dachau and Sobibor. The weary refugees were like those who clogged the roads of Central and Eastern Europe when Nazi armies began their advances in 1939. The subtext was clear: Milosevic was a monster of the magnitude of Hitler. The refugees were being implicitly compared to the Jews in the Holocaust.

I can see how these terrible images might induce such thoughts. And I can also see why politicians on both sides of this conflict would seek to invoke the memory of the greatest evil of our century. There is no greater stigma, no more useful propaganda tool, than to label your enemy as a modern-day Hitler. But I think it is wrong and takes us into dangerous territory.

What is happening now in Kosovo is undoubtedly evil. Nobody who has spent any time talking with refugees and hearing their stories over the past fortnight could avoid the conclusion that they are the victims of evil. I spent all day last Saturday sitting and taking detailed statements from people who had just been driven from their homes. They told a similar story of masked thugs and five-minute warnings to leave. Everything they owned had been stolen from them. There was evidence, too, of murder and rape.

But the expulsion of the Albanians from Kosovo is not comparable to the Holocaust. It is useful to remember the facts of the Holocaust: six million dead Jews; the attempt to wipe off the face of the earth an entire race of people; a network of camps with gas chambers and crematoria whose sole purpose was the industrialized destruction of world Jewry.

It was a singular event, the crime of crimes. It was a project spurred by racial hatred, and one to which all other war aims were considered secondary. The Nazi leaders were true believers and did not allow any diplomatic, much less humane, considerations to enter into the equation. They did not merely want the Jews out of Germany, they wanted them obliterated from history. The only remotely comparable event in recent history has been the Rwandan genocide. Then, nearly a million people were slaughtered in an attempt to destroy the Tutsi ethnic group. Again, the plan was for a systematic and methodical destruction of an entire race. And, like the Holocaust, it very nearly worked.

I was talking about this with a Jewish colleague who happened to be with me in Macedonia reporting on the refugee crisis. His own grandparents had escaped out of Germany but numerous close relatives were later murdered in the camps. Like me, he was horrified by the plight of the refugees but also uneasy – in fact rather angry – at the constant invoking of the Holocaust. 'They are two very different things. Both were wrong but both were very different. If Milosevic were like Hitler he would want to kill every single Albanian,' he said.

My colleague pointed to the Nazis' expulsion of German Jews to Poland in 1938 – before the Final Solution had been fully thought through – as a more apt comparison. I would suggest that Stalin's vast population-clearances in the Caucasus or his action against the Cossacks would be an even more appropriate comparison.

For Milosevic, like Stalin, is a ruthless and cunning tactician. He uses terror and state power precisely to further his own power; he shares the megalomaniacal paranoia of the Soviet leader but he has chosen (I use the word advisedly; there is nothing instinctual in his embrace of Serb patriotism) nationalism and not Communism as the vehicle by which he will retain power. In the way that the classical Leninist ideas of political organization offered Stalin an alibi – if he needed one – for holding absolute power, then Serb chauvinism, motivated by fear and a sense of victimhood, has provided Milosevic with his means of survival.

But I somehow doubt that Mr Milosevic cares one way or the other about the survival of the Albanian race. He first used the Kosovo Albanians as a tactical weapon to create a political power-base built on Serb fear. Now he is driving them into exile to alter the balance of population inside Kosovo and to embarrass the NATO governments that have launched military action against him. It is worth noting that plans to drive the Albanians from Kosovo long pre-date Mr Milosevic. They were drawn up in earnest in the thirties, but the outbreak of the Second World War and the coming to power of Tito forced the abandonment of those plans. There have certainly been acts of genocide inside Kosovo: people have been murdered solely because of their ethnic background. The removal and destruction of identity documents and the 'cleansing' of people from their traditional lands involves a form of genocide.

But there is no sign of a plan to wipe out the Kosovo Albanians as a people, no Final Solution to the Kosovo Albanian problem. I don't doubt that such sentiments exist in the wilder heart of Serb nationalism, but Mr Milosevic is concerned primarily with his own power and not with a fanatical racial crusade of the kind that made Hitler such a singular figure of evil.

What is happening in Kosovo is bad enough without having to resort to inaccurate and emotive historical comparisons. Let the leaders of today be judged for the crimes of today by the standards of today. By comparing the events of the past fortnight with Nazi Germany, we not only deny the awful singularity of the Holocaust but we reduce ourselves to the realm of absurd comparison. That in a sense removes from Milosevic his personal responsibility for what is happening now. He becomes just another demon on to whose features we paint the little moustache and scrawl the swastika.

It is bad history and it makes for bad politics. Let us analyse and describe Milosevic in the context in which he belongs: he is another dictator who will manipulate ethnic chauvinism and apply terror when he needs to, but he is certainly no Hitler. That, of course, is not a statement of absolution; it does not mitigate the evil that has been visited upon the Kosovo Albanians. It is merely a plea for a man to be judged for his own crimes and not those of another.

CULTURE SHOCK IN CHIANTISHIRE

Tuscany, June 1999

Hundreds of thousands of refugees were streaming out of Kosovo
into neighbouring countries. All had stories to tell of ethnic
cleansing and brutality. After several weeks of providing news
coverage from the scene, the author was able to rejoin his wife and
son for a holiday across the Adriatic in Italy. But not even the
beauties of the Tuscan countryside and the warmth and
friendliness of its people were able to banish from his mind the
images of suffering from Kosovo.

Just above Greve, where the vineyards and olive groves climb,
one above the other toward the horizon, the walls of the Villa
Vignamaggio glowed pink and welcoming in the late spring sunlight. I rolled down the window of the hire car and breathed in
the country air, warm and heavy with the hint of rain. We had
been told to expect thunder and lightning soon, a typical Tuscan
spring the man in the café had said. In the back a small child was
dozing, beside me my wife plotted the last few miles of the journey
on the map. It was a fairly typical scene from an ordinary European
holiday. And yet I was having some difficulty adjusting to the
circumstances, to the difference between Tuscany and the place I
had just come from. There was no long line of tractors here; no
vast tented cities; no smell of human waste; no terrible stories of
death and dispossession. I think the phrase 'culture shock' barely
begins to describe the acute sense of 'difference' I felt.

And then I chided myself for such self-indulgence. 'Culture
shock'? I hardly knew the meaning of the word. As we crossed
the gravel courtyard of the Villa Vignamaggio I tried to imagine
what it would be like if one moment you lived in a house of your

own, surrounded by your family, and then minutes later you found yourself crammed on to a train or a tractor or struggling on foot, driven by gunmen away from everything you held precious. That is 'culture shock' – the expulsion from the world of the rooted and secure; coming from where we do, from the Europe we live in, it is difficult, if not impossible to imagine an experience as violent or oppressive.

But in Tuscany I was doing my best not to think too much about all of this. The idea was a total break from the Balkans. Time with family, some good books and good food and wine. But soon enough I realized that Italy is quite the wrong place to go to escape the Balkans. That evening, while I stood on the terrace of the Villa Vignamaggio, glass in hand as I admired the last streaks of sunlight, two jets appeared, flying in formation overhead. I don't know whose aircraft they were or what mission they were on but they were military jets and it is possible they were returning from the skies over Kosovo. As they flew into the distance, two thin vapour trails hung in the evening sky. It was as if the god of war had been standing on a Tuscan hillside and reached up to scrape his fingernail across the crimson fabric of the sky. Later that night the promised thunder and lightning came but below it, as night gave way to dawn, I swore I heard the far-off roar of jets.

In the nearby village of L'Amola, I was told that a family of Kosovo refugees had recently passed through. The sight of the mother and her seven young children, worn out and hungry after their flight, had prompted locals to raise a collection. There had been a generous response and, as Maria the waitress in the restaurant told us, it prompted a lot of discussion about the war. 'You don't really understand what it is like until you see these people, until you hear what they have been through,' she said. And I agreed. There is nothing that quite prepares one for the destitution and wretchedness of people who look so much like us. Here in Tuscany I found a great deal more sympathy for the Kosovo Albanians than I'd been led to believe existed. There is, it is true, a lot of wariness in Italy about this war, a fear that it could send chaos and thousands of refugees flooding across the Adriatic. The Italians, along with the Greeks, have been historically suspicious of Albanians, tending to write them off as criminals or spongers.

But in the small villages of Chianti I found something rather different. Here the televised images of Albanian suffering have offended something central to the Italian identity: the love of family and the particular reverence for children. As Maria said in the Restaurant L'Amola: 'You see it as if they were your children or as if it were your parents who were being treated like that.' After a few days I knew that I was foolish to imagine I could forget Kosovo, that I could shut out the war. Italy was too close to Kosovo for that and the concern of its people too real to simply shut oneself away among the vineyards; and nor was it possible to watch the warm indulgence shown to my own child by a succession of Italians, without remembering the countless faces of exhausted children I'd seen a few days before, struggling along the dusty roads of exile.

WAR'S END

London, May 1999

After weeks of NATO bombing, a peace agreement was signed at a meeting of NATO and Serb generals. The war was over. The policies of President Clinton and Prime Minister Blair had proved to be effective. And a partnership with the people of the Balkans was just beginning.

I was wrong. Two weeks ago I wrote that a ground war seemed inevitable. I didn't believe that the air campaign alone would force Milosevic to move. I didn't believe his troops would leave Kosovo unless there were NATO troops to drive them out. Well he buckled and surrendered (that is what has happened, however Belgrade may try to dress it up) and I join the long list of commentators who at different points in this conflict failed to appreciate the impact of the air campaign on the Yugoslav leadership. I did always believe (and say) that he would be defeated — I just didn't imagine it could be done with aircraft alone.

Now that the bombers and missiles have done their work and the Serbs are on their way out of Kosovo, my friends 'Easy' and Arber and their families will be getting ready to leave Albania and go home. I am happy for them and for the hundreds of thousands of other refugees who were driven out by the Serb warlord. 'Easy' will get to have his big celebration party in Mitrovica sometime in the next few months and I might just be able to keep my promise and be there with him. As I have said several times before, no people were more deserving of Western support and compassion than the Kosovo Albanians.

I read a great deal from the anti-war side about this being a war of NATO expansionism, a war about the consolidation of American power on the borders of Russia, an attempt to define an aggressive new world order. It was none of that and those who peddled that line failed to see beyond their own reflexive anti-Americanism.

Many of them were still trapped in an old leftist time-warp where Yankee power romped through South-East Asia and Latin America. Instead of the reticent Clinton and his reluctant generals they saw Nixon and Kissinger and Dr Strangelove; they saw Ronald Reagan and his Contras and the malign tentacles of the Military Industrial Complex. They protested about the need for UN resolutions while forgetting the scores of them Milosevic had already ignored; they turned a blind eye to the years of Serb promise-breaking and double-dealing and acted as if Milosevic was a man we could 'do business with'. (In this of course they were no different from the American and European diplomats who for years fostered the illusion that Milosevic was the guarantor of stability in the region.)

Others were blinded by their own bitterness about America's relentless and often unjust support for the Israelis in the Middle East and refused to see any possibility that the United States might in this case be capable of acting in a good cause and actually succeeding. Sure the American record in the Middle East is appallingly one-sided but in Kosovo the White House got it right. It defies logic to suggest that because America gets it wrong in one part of the world, it is incapable of getting it right anywhere else. The US support for Croatia and the ethnic cleansing of the Krajina Serbs is also cited as an example of disgracefully one-sided behaviour. Yes, it was. And yes, Tudjman should be investigated for his responsibility for war crimes in the Krajina and Bosnia-Herzegovina. But please don't tell me that any of this makes it wrong for the Clinton White House to draw a line in the sand and stand up for the cause of justice in Kosovo. It may not feel nice, it may look like hypocrisy. But it was the right thing to do.

This war was not about NATO expansionism, still less about the arrogant flexing of Yankee muscle. The truth of this age is that we battle to keep the Americans interested in what happens in the rest of the world. They are a people whose political and military establishment has a deep isolationist streak and whose broader population are hugely ignorant of the world beyond American shores. For these reasons we find ourselves in a position not of restraining American power but having to endlessly confront the US with the moral imperative of humanitarian intervention. Remember that for the one hundred days of this century's most recent genocide (in Rwanda) the Americans twisted and wriggled and did everything they could not to become involved; how they haggled over the rental terms for armoured vehicles for the UN force. Anything to avoid being dragged into a conflict in a far-away country. At the end of it all nearly a million people were dead, thanks in no small measure to Washington's absolute refusal to countenance action. This time the Yanks did the decent thing. Not without a lot of prodding and pressure from Blair, mind you, but the right thing all the same.

It was, as Tony Blair said at the very outset, a war against the evil of ethnic cleansing. In the course of the war brutal and stupid things were done by NATO. Innocent people were killed. But do not try to pin the blame for the great crime of the war – the deportation of hundreds of thousands of people – on the Western allies. Don't forget that in the year before the war Milosevic's men had driven some three hundred thousand people out of their homes in Kosovo, that Serb murder squads were touring the countryside butchering civilians, and that for decades Serb extremists had nurtured a plan for the expulsion of the Kosovo Albanians. Milosevic used the NATO bombing as a convenient pretext for emptying the province of its majority population. But they left at the point of Serbian guns – not because of NATO air strikes.

War is profoundly troubling to the liberal conscience. As I have written before, it ruptures our idea of ourselves: it is an abomination, a defiler of conscience and body and soul. You do not have to walk among the dead and maimed or to record their stories to realize this. But after ten years of the evil wrought by ethnic war in the Balkans did we have a choice this time around? I honestly believe not. We are coming to the end of one era in the Balkans. Soon enough Milosevic and Tudjman will no longer be in power, the minor warlords who grew up around them have been sent a terrible warning and we at last seem to be engaged with the region in a real and committed sense. Political inertia, diplomatic fudge and double-dealing, moral abandonment, pious wishful thinking – these are the qualities which until now defined our attempts to deal with this bloodstained territory. The tramping feet of refugees, the acres of shattered ground have put an end to that.

Sooner or later Kosovo itself will move towards independence. The idea that ninety per cent of the people of a region can be forcibly compelled to live under the sovereignty of a state they loathe is simply untenable – it is only possible where state terror is practised at its most absolute, say in East Timor or Burma. I hope the KLA realizes that it is in its interests to work with NATO and not to try and subvert the peace by launching a renewed war against the Serbs from liberated territory. And if NATO itself is to have any credibility as a guarantor of peace it must act ruthlessly against those who will want to wreak vengeance on Serb civilians. The allies did not fight a war against ethnic cleansing only to precipitate the expulsion of the Kosovo Serbs. The Serbs may not want to remain but they deserve the protection of NATO if they wish to try.

In broader terms we need to be ready for the crisis which will erupt in Serbia itself soon. Neighbouring Montenegro is also fearfully unstable. We are, as has been repeatedly said in recent days, simply at the beginning of our partnership with the people of the Balkans. And that is what it is: not an overlordship or a dictatorship but a partnership. Never again can we afford – morally or practically – to look the other way or encourage, through our weakness and vacillation, the whims of dictators.

Part Three

FROM IRELAND

WHERE WE CAME FROM

Dublin, June 1999

In the early summer of 1999, Northern Ireland's old foes appeared to be inching closer to peace. It was a time for reflection for Irish people north and south of the border, and for taking a fresh look at the island's brutal history.

It was an election campaign which promised to be as bitter as any ever fought in Listowel. On one side Fianna Fail, the party of De Valera and militant Irish nationalism; on the other, Fine Gael, the party which descended from Michael Collins and those who had voted for the partition of Ireland in 1922. Looming over both was the shadow of the Catholic Church, an institution of unrivalled power in Listowel as in most other southern towns. Both parties paid obeisance to the church. Both doffed their caps to the priests. But if moral issues (in Ireland that usually meant anything to do with sex) were not involved the priests tended to stay in the background during elections. And, like every campaign since partition, the election of 1951 was dominated by the politics of the civil war. The stuff which was kept under wraps most of the time came flooding out in elections: who had fought on what side, who had killed whom, who had really represented the will of the Irish people.

Both sides were limbering up for an orgy of bile and insults. Enter my uncle John B. Keane and a group of subversive associates. Sick to death of the old bitterness they decided to take matters into their own hands and put up a non-party candidate. He was the inestimable and unimpeachable Thomas Doodle Esq. Needless to say, Tom Doodle did not exist. In reality he was a friend of my uncle's who was persuaded to disguise himself and play the part for the duration of the campaign. At first the main parties were inclined to ignore the Doodle campaign. The work of young lads with nothing better to do. And then came the Doodle monster meeting. Those who were present remember it as the biggest meeting in the town since Parnell came in the last century. Crowds pressed around the railway station where my uncle and his friends were waiting with a horse-drawn carriage to meet the candidate. As he emerged a brass band began to play and somebody in the crowd fired several celebratory shots into the air.

Followed by several hundred people Doodle and his spin doctors proceeded to the market square where he unveiled his daring manifesto to rescue Ireland from civil-war politics. The promises were intentionally ludicrous. The crowd knew this and cheered him on wildly. On jobs he pledged to open a factory for shaving the hair off gooseberries; there was also a hint of universal free drink. Crucially he promised 'that every man would have more than the next'. In the atmosphere of political clientelism and unrealistic promises which prevailed at the time, the crowd delighted in the biting satire. The meeting finished with the ringing campaign slogan: 'Vote the Noodle and give the whole Kaboodle to Doodle.' To orgiastic cheering Doodle vanished into the night.

In the event Doodle did not stand in the election. His candidacy was a joke, but a very pointed one. Spare us your old hatreds, the young were saying, we want a different Ireland. My uncle would later carry on the battle as one of Ireland's best loved writers, satirizing the croney politics of the day and portraying in his plays a country struggling for social and political change. In the sixties he was one of the leaders of a movement which would argue against the compulsory teaching of Irish in schools. Although a fluent speaker and lover of Irish, John B. felt the young were being turned against the language. He had little time for the narrow nationalist elite who used the language as a political weapon. It was a stand which would earn him verbal and physical abuse, culminating in a savage attack at a meeting in Dublin from which he was lucky to escape without serious injury.

FROM IRELAND

I only heard the story of Tom Doodle in its full glory last summer in the course of a long journey back through the political landscape of my childhood and family. I knew that various members of my father's family had been involved in the IRA, among them my grandmother Hannie Purtill.

Once while staying with her in Kerry during the holidays I remember a war pension arriving at her house on Church Street. And when I asked her about it she admitted she'd once been an IRA volunteer. But like so many who had taken part in the bitter struggles of 1919–22, Hannie was slow to talk about what had happened, what she had seen and done. I knew only that she was a devout follower of Michael Collins and that after the Treaty she had abandoned the gun in favour of politics. Throughout my life I had known her as a gentle granny, a woman who passionately supported constitutional politics and never neglected to cast her vote. And so when my uncle told me about her revolutionary life one morning last summer, I knew I was discovering an altogether more complex woman.

At the age of seventeen Hannie had become a member of Cumann Na Mban, the female wing of the IRA. The women provided intelligence, logistical and moral support to the gunmen who were attacking British forces and the Royal Irish Constabulary. My grand-uncle, Mick Purtill (Hannie's brother), was one of the main IRA leaders in the area. One of Hannie's jobs was to smuggle guns around the neighbourhood. According to my uncle she did this by concealing them in her underwear, a place not even the notorious Black and Tans (British Irregulars) would think of searching. But they did suspect her enough to issue a death threat. One evening while she was walking home, a Black and Tan by the name of Darcy stopped Hannie and put a gun to her head. She was given twenty-four hours to get out of town, a warning she chose to ignore. Hannie survived but many of her comrades-in-arms did not. Hannie was no different from thousands of young men and women who had flocked to the Republican movement

91

after the British had executed the leaders of the Easter 1916 Rebellion. In a matter of weeks British stupidity had inflamed public opinion. As my uncle put it to me: 'If you have never had to aspire for freedom, if you have always had it, then it's impossible to understand what it means to live without it.'

The war of independence in North Kerry was a savage affair. The nearby town of Ballylongford was attacked and burned by the Black and Tans; in the valley of Knockanure the Tans shot dead three men after ordering them to run across an open field. My grand-uncle helped the only survivor of that attack to escape and bring the story to national attention. For its part the IRA conducted a ruthless campaign, killing Black and Tans and also fellow Irishmen who wore the uniform of the Royal Irish Constabulary. Houses belonging to unpopular Protestant landlords were burned, those suspected of pro-British sympathies were killed or driven out, informers were executed without mercy. In one case an RIC district inspector was walking up Church Street in Listowel after attending mass when he was surprised by the IRA and murdered. I don't know how much of the local campaign my grandmother participated in or how much she knew about the planning of such attacks. I do remember my father telling me a story about a murdered British officer haunting the house on Church Street, a green shadow flickering across the walls at night. Was this the fruit of fantasy or did it hint at some dark story untold? My grandmother died before I was interested enough to ask her about the truth of those days. I will never know. So much of our Irish past is snagged with myth and suppressed memory, it is as if the blood and the bitterness made truth too painful to bear.

When the British departed in 1922 the IRA split. My grand-mother took the side of the pro-Treaty forces. In North Kerry the civil war was, in the words of Professor Brendan Kenneally, a family friend and a leading Irish poet: 'The dirtiest fight of all time, families split by it, football teams split by it. A bitter, bitter time.' Two short stories he remembers from that time: at Ballyseedy outside the town of Tralee, soldiers of the Free State army tied nine IRA prisoners to a landmine and then stood back and detonated the device. Eight of the men were blown to pieces. One miraculously survived to tell the story. At Clashmelcon near Listowel a group of IRA men hiding in caves overlooking the sea were urged to surrender and climb up some ropes which had been lowered by the army. As they came to the top the soldiers cut the ropes and sent the men falling to their deaths on the rocks below. That was Irishmen killing Irishmen. Irish Catholics killing Irish Catholics. I did not hear those stories while I was growing up. The history I learned in school was safe history: Irish heroes and English villains.

And there was no shortage of English villainy to contemplate. The curse of Cromwell, the rebellion of 1798, the famine, the Easter Rising, the Black and Tans. But the blood and guts of what we did to each other was skipped over. The civil war and the bloody reality of what the IRA did in prosecuting its war against the British were glossed over. I went to school in 1966, the year Ireland celebrated the fiftieth anniversary of the Easter Rising. They were stirring times. I remember the radio relentlessly playing ballads and martial music. As the voice of one announcer droned repeatedly: 'If you must sing a song, sing an Irish song.' I dreamed of dying for Ireland. Our schoolyard battles were always the same: the Irish versus the Brits. My hero was Patrick Pearse. Noble and handsome. I longed to emulate him, to perish in glorious battle. And I understood too that to be Irish was to be Catholic. I may have loathed the boredom of Sunday masses but my Catholic identity was not up for debate. It had come down to me from my devout grandmother, who had in turn been given it by her grandparents.

But looking back now I sense that 1966 was the high-water mark of the old nationalism. The Irish identity which had been defined in terms of its Catholic faith and its antagonism to the British was evolving into something altogether more exciting. We might have played war games in the day but at night we had television to look at with its imported programmes and ideas.

We were heading into Europe, taking part in UN peacekeeping operations, we were embarking on economic policies that reversed the isolationism of the past. My uncle John B. and many other writers were challenging the accepted orthodoxies of church and state. The women's movement was agitating on issues like contraception and equal rights in the workplace. All around me Ireland was changing, but I was too young to see it.

I do have one memory which underlines both the nature of the state and the challenge it was facing. Every few weeks my mother would hand me a brown envelope and send me to Mrs Gleeson's chemist around the corner from our Dublin home. Once inside I would hand the envelope to the chemist on duty. She would disappear into a back room and return with the envelope, filled now with small tablets. 'What's that, Mam?' I asked one morning. 'That's just the pill, love. Just the pill.' I hadn't a clue what 'the pill' was but I knew it was something secret. And there it was, a small act of subversion but one doubtless being repeated by women across the country. It was a new revolution, altogether different from the battles of the past.

And then in 1969 the long festering wound of partition burst in our faces. The politics of blood returned to Ireland and filled our television screens every night. As the Troubles ground on, we were by turn horrified, outraged, sickened, mystified, saddened, apathetic. The struggle which my grandmother and her comrades had abandoned in 1922 in favour of constitutional politics had come back to haunt us. At first we felt sympathy for the northerners, our nationalist impulses twitched reflexively. But the war up north was brutal and unromantic. Dismembered bodies. Widows and orphans. We didn't live through it, but its poison infected the whole island. And with every brutal image it became harder to cling to the simplistic, nationalist pieties. To paraphrase Yeats: Romantic Ireland was dead and gone. It took thirty years of murder and violent sectarianism to bring the people of Ireland, north and south, to the point of agreement. And now that we have reached that point, there is a feeling akin to a collective intake of breath. We hover before this peace, uncertain and nervous. Will it last? Where will it take us? What kind of country have we become on the journey to peace? I don't know what my grandmother would think of this new island. I suspect the conservative Catholic part of her nature would find some of the changes difficult to accept. But I hope the revolutionary in her, the rebel heart, would celebrate the freedom we are finding.

GLAD, SO GLAD TO
BE WRONG

Belfast, April 1998

It was the moment many Irish men and women thought would never come: the signing of a peace accord, called 'The Good Friday Agreement', which was designed to bring the long violent years of 'the Troubles' to an end.

Never have I been so glad to be wrong. Until the very last moment I doubted that a deal could be reached. Shaped by my island's bloody history and steeped in native pessimism, I could not believe that an accommodation between Orange and Green was possible. And so when friends from abroad asked what I thought of the peace process, I would caution them against hope; there was too much bad blood from the past for this to end in smiles, I said. How wrong I was, how wonderfully wrong.

I come from an Irish generation for whom the Troubles were the defining political experience of our lives. Certainly as a southern Catholic I did not have to experience the daily round of bombings and killings. That was happening up the road, a distant menacing rumble that occasionally exploded into our lives. But like everybody else who grew up on the island – Catholic, Protestant and non-believer – I felt the burden of our history. Ireland is simply too small a place to be able to escape completely the poisonous breath of the past.

From my earliest days I was taught that the English were our oppressors, that our nation was incomplete while the six counties of Ulster remained under the Union flag. My parents too had learned this tune and their parents before them. Grandparents on both sides of my family had taken part in the war of independence against the British. The prevailing political ethos told us that an

Ireland divided could never be at peace. As for the Ulster Protestants who were supposed to be my fellow countrymen – I regarded them as obdurate and bigoted. I never could see their point of view.

Up north the children of Protestant Ulster were learning another tune. They were taught to fear us and regard us as foreigners. We were portrayed as citizens of a priest-ridden and backward country. To them a United Ireland meant domination by Papists and the loss of their Protestant faith and identity. The Catholics alongside whom they lived were to be despised and kept from power. Discrimination and exclusion were the order of the day. The Ulster Catholics were the enemy within, the fifth columnists waiting to open the city gates for their brethren from the south.

And then, in the mid-nineties, I went to live in Belfast. My work took me into Catholic and Protestant ghettos, to the funerals of IRA men and of police officers, to the marches of hardline Loyalists and die-hard Republicans. My eyes were opened to a reality that those who live outside Ulster can never really understand.

The Nobel prize-winning poet Seamus Heaney coined the chilling phrase 'each neighbourly murder' to describe the nature of Ulster's killing. For this was a war fought out between people who passed each other in the street every day, families who had lived alongside each other for generations. This was not killing by remote control but up close and very personal. Here compromise was the dirtiest word. It meant betrayal and on both sides the traitor was the most despicable creature.

It was the funerals which put an end to any simplistic ideas I might have had about Irish unity. I soon realized that the people of the south had not the remotest sense of what their fellow islanders were suffering. The pain and suspicion and fear were just across the border from us but Ulster might as well have been another planet. After nearly three decades of violence I sensed that the two parts of the island were psychologically further apart than ever before. And so, devoid of hope, I left Ulster and went to

South Africa to observe that country's remarkable transition to democracy.

While Mandela and de Klerk swept towards a new dispensation, the news from home was depressingly familiar: shootings, bombings, bigotry. Watching the South African leaders in action I despaired of their counterparts in Ireland. But living far away I did not realize that great changes were taking place in Ulster. For the first time in recent Irish history, the leaders of Sinn Fein and the IRA were telling their supporters that negotiation might offer a way forward. On the Protestant side there was a growing acceptance of the need for an agreed solution. The politics of siege would no longer suffice. The ordinary people had never seemed so weary of conflict, more desiring of a settlement.

Now that the deal has been done, we know that there are dangerous times ahead. The forces of bigotry and fear will do their best to destroy our new-found sense of hope. They cannot be allowed to succeed. The main political leaders have all shown exemplary courage. It is now up to the people – north and south – to support them and create an Ireland where our children can live free from the tribal hatreds of the past. The poet Louis MacNeice, an Ulster Protestant, once wrote of the long struggle: 'There will be sunlight later.' Today I can see the first glorious rays.

THE KILLING OF THE QUINNS

Belfast, July 1998

Hardline Protestants were encamped at Drumcree in defence of their right to take part in traditional marches, some of them through Republican areas. And Protestant extremists were being blamed for a firebomb attack on a house in Ballymoney in which three young boys were killed.

I had planned to write about something different this time. I feared that three consecutive weeks devoted to Northern Ireland might begin to look like a columnist's monomania. But after the week we have been through, after the horror of Ballymoney and the subsequent collapse of Drumcree, I know there is nothing else I want to write about. It was the week the tribalists sickened us with murder, the week of bitter in-fighting and weasel words, the week of hatred and tears, and above all, the most important week since the Troubles began.

Those who have reported Northern Ireland down the years know better than to create a pecking order of atrocities. There should be no league table of cruelty. Bloody Sunday, Bloody Friday, the fireball of La Mon House, Enniskillen, the Shankhill Butchers. The list of horror would take pages to recall. There are more than three thousand deaths – each one a story of pain for somebody.

And yet I sense that with the murders of the three Quinn boys some terrible watershed has been passed. What kind of island is this, we ask, where children burn for the madness of adults?

I guess that is a question many of the Orangemen at Drumcree were asking themselves as they packed up to go home. As one of them put it to me, simply: 'I am sick to my heart.'

There was something tired and defeated about most of the Orangemen I spoke to this week. They were shocked by the murders, it is true. But the overriding impression is one of confusion. There was simply no map for this situation, and no amount of spin from David Jones or Ian Paisley about the 'real' cause of the murders was going to make them feel any better. Jones battled frantically all week to keep the cause alive, ploughing on with remarkable insensitivity while the majority of Orangemen deserted the cause of Drumcree in their droves.

I spent the week in a small town in West Tyrone, close to the border with the Irish Republic. This is a place where Protestants have long felt themselves besieged by the forces of nationalism. Out there on the fringe of the Union, Protestants have always understood the imperative of group solidarity.

But Drumcree and the Quinn murders have changed everything. The Unionist family here, as in so much of the province, is more divided than it has ever been.

Throughout the week local moderates have been publicly abused. The word 'traitor' is regularly shouted at pro-Trimble politicians. But for once in the history of Unionism, that bitter epithet has lost its powerful resonance. We know that the only betrayal now is on the part of those willing to threaten the hope of peace for the cause of tribalism.

To many people in Britain the language and principles of hardline Orangeism are incomprehensible. After the Quinn murders, I suspect the majority of British people have moved from being perplexed by the rituals to feeling profound antipathy towards the Order's actions.

The cause of the Union, to which people like David Jones swear such loyalty, has been badly damaged. If the mainlanders had little enough time for the idea of a British Ulster, they have far less now.

And yet I am not in the least mystified by the actions and words of people like David Jones or Joel Patten, the leader of the hardline Spirit of Drumcree group. When Patten hurled abuse and brandished his brolly at moderate Orangemen earlier this week, he saw himself as a defender of the faith and the Protestant people.

You may find that extraordinary, but don't for a moment doubt his sincerity.

Four years ago I spent several weeks in Joel Patten's company. I was making a film about Protestant identity. One evening, coming towards the end of our filming, Joel produced a set of maps and set them out on a coffee table. The maps showed the streets of a small Armagh village from which Joel believed Protestants were being ethnically cleansed by the IRA.

He had colour-coded each building according to religion. If memory serves me well, the Catholic houses were green, the Protestant ones blue. The green shade was spreading, annexing Protestant territory. As Joel outlined the various murders of Protestants that had taken place, I had the feeling that I was listening to a conversation from the seventeenth century: the fearful planter surrounded by the wily, hostile natives.

We walked around the town, Joel pointing out the buildings that had been 'lost' to the Catholics. He showed me his local Orange Hall, recently firebombed by nationalists.

The final part of our film involved a debate between Joel and some of his colleagues and a group of Catholics from the south. Most of the southerners had never travelled north before. When Joel came to meet them, he conspicuously avoided shaking hands. The debate was reasonably civil and relaxed until I asked one of the southerners if he accepted Joel's right to be British. His answer was immediate and blunt: 'If you are born on the island of Ireland you are Irish. They are Irish.'

Joel immediately erupted. 'You see. There it is. Just what I have been trying to explain. You are trying to tell me what my identity is,' he snapped. The argument went on and on, with no hint of accommodation on either side. And yet when it finished I remember Joel standing and drinking tea with the southerners. By no stretch of the imagination could one say he was friendly towards them, but he did stay and talk and listen.

In the wake of Drumcree it is hard to imagine Joel Patten or any other hardliner agreeing to drink tea with southern Catholics, let alone discuss the future of Ulster with them. The hardline faction will not have been given cause for doubt or self-questioning by the events of the past week. If anything, they will regard themselves as more put upon, more righteous in their cause.

When I ran into Joel in the field at Drumcree, he told me the march along the Garvaghy Road was a make-or-break issue for Protestants. And he made no secret of the fact that David Trimble was his ultimate target. Joel's candour convinced me that Drumcree was as much about destroying the moderates as it was about a sacred right to march.

The hardliners have suffered a serious defeat at Drumcree, but they will not go away. Already they are preparing for the next big battle: the decommissioning of paramilitary weapons.

This is an issue which strikes a much deeper chord with the Protestant community than the right to march down the Garvaghy Road. It is an issue on which Trimble cannot afford to be seen to concede. The courage he showed in calling for the Orangemen to quit Drumcree will have its price. One pro-Trimble Assemblyman told me the Ulster Unionists would be committing suicide if they went into government with Sinn Fein without some real movement on decommissioning. 'There is no way I or anybody else who is pro-agreement could back David on that,' he said.

I believe him. If Trimble were to back down on decommissioning, an already divided party would more than likely collapse, bringing the Assembly down with it.

And so the focus swings back to Gerry Adams and Martin McGuinness. Giving any credit to Unionists may be difficult for them, but they must surely recognize Trimble's courage. If they can go one step further and encourage the IRA to make a practical gesture on decommissioning then the moderates on the Unionist side will be able to ignore the bitter taunts of 'traitor'. And without Trimble and his moderates there is no solution, only a return to the sectarian swamp.

THE DAY OF THE BUTCHERS

Omagh, August 1998

**A huge bomb explosion which shattered the centre of Omagh
appeared to threaten the peace process in Northern Ireland. But, as
the dust settled, it became clear that the blast had marked a
watershed in the Republican movement and had further
marginalized the extremists.**

The time of the butchers is passing. You may find that hard to
believe on this sad Monday, but I ask you to make an act of faith.
Not one based on wishful thinking or utopian dreaming; simply
an acknowledgement of the long distance that has been travelled
in a very short time.

The killers who planned and planted the Omagh bomb are the
leftovers of the Troubles; the poisoned dregs of thirty years of
violence. They are not the here and now but belong instead to the
vanishing Ireland of closed minds and fanatical hearts.

I am fond of quoting Yeats in relation to this peace process,
only because I believe he was a better social historian than any of
our academics. And so, when I imagine the obscenity of an
eighteen-month-old baby blasted to death, I turn to 'The Second
Coming':

> *The blood dimmed tide is loosed, and everywhere*
> *The ceremony of innocence is drowned;*
> *The best lack all conviction, while the worst*
> *Are full of passionate intensity.*

But I do not quote these lines in despair. Rather, I am trying to
illustrate how far we have travelled from the divided Ireland
so powerfully evoked by Yeats. There was a time when the

103

hate-mongers and tribalists were the only show in town, a time when the 'best' did truly seem ground down, reduced to fuzzy platitudes but unwilling to forge the path to peace. Those days are gone, and we should not let Omagh – for all its horror – convince us otherwise.

I admit that my first reaction when the news came on was to say: 'God help this bloody country.' My second reaction was to feel deep anger; the kind of anger that makes you lose perspective. There will be many people in Northern Ireland and the south who will want a swift and ruthless response from the security forces. The cries of: 'Send in the SAS' or 'Intern the bastards' are already being heard. Fair enough. It is hard to blame those who have suffered so much.

But if ever there were a time for calm nerves, this is it. Ruthless counter-insurgency operations and internment might work . . . for a while. In the long run, however, they would simply feed the grievance that drives groups like the Real IRA, Continuity IRA and the INLA.

Any crackdown by the security forces in the north or south will simply give the dissidents an issue around which to rally support. What works is not the sudden and dramatic imposition of emergency rule. Rather, it is the slow and painstaking business of intelligence-gathering and interception. The vastly improved security co-operation between the north and south has already prevented a large number of dissident operations. After Omagh, that co-operation can only increase. The people have already spoken. The bunch of lunatics responsible for Omagh cannot be allowed to drag us backwards.

My own suspicion is that the Omagh bombing has put the dissidents so far beyond the pale that they have become more than an embarrassment to the mainstream Republican movement. They are now a potentially murderous threat.

The Real IRA and its associates regard Gerry Adams and Martin McGuinness as traitors, in much the same way that an earlier generation of Republicans saw Michael Collins as the enemy of Irish unity.

Adams has not forgotten the fate of Collins, but he must know that he and the rest of Ireland's political leaders have a mandate that would have been unimaginable in Collins' time: a vote by all the people of Ireland to work together in peace.

That is what counts. In the south, we ended the campaign by republican die-hards in 1923 by jailing and shooting. It was a ruthless and bloody campaign when legal norms and niceties were cast aside and scores of Republicans were executed. The bitterness left over from that period has only begun to vanish with this generation.

Mr Adams is now confronted by a dilemma similar to that faced by Collins. His former comrades-in-arms are continuing a war that the vast majority of the people simply do not want. The temptation may be for the mainstream Republicans to turn their guns on the dissidents and finish them off in much the same way as Collins did in the Irish civil war.

This may be tempting, but it is wrong. The last thing we need now is a bloody Republican feud. We are now involved in a peace process. Leave the business of dealing with these 'bitter-enders' to the legally instituted authorities.

What has been infinitely more valuable are the statements of condemnation from Adams and McGuinness. To those who have become used to their equivocation and dodging down the years, the swift denunciations represent a true step forward.

But actions do speak louder than words. And so in the wake of Omagh we all need to hear that the war is over, that punishment attacks and intimidation are over, that guns and bombs are being put down for ever. Otherwise, the condemnation means nothing.

I began by saying that the time of the butchers was passing. A month ago we mourned the death of the three Quinn boys in Ballymoney. That savage burning marked a watershed in Loyalism.

Omagh represents a similar moment in the history of Republican-ism. Cold comfort, you might say, to the individuals whose lives and homes have been torn apart by these atrocities. Nothing can conjure smiles and laughter from broken bodies.

But amid the weeping we can see emerging a people determined to set the power of hope against the fearful claims of history; a people who have made a choice that the bombers would never understand, a choice that is fundamentally about good and evil. Welcome to the country of the good.

SAVING PRIVATE DALY

London, January 1999

Private James Joseph Daly was an Irishman fighting in the British army in India. In 1920 he was taken before an army court accused of leading a mutiny. He was found guilty and was executed by firing squad. Justice was seen to have been done. But was the young soldier really treated fairly?

Most of you will never have heard of Private James Joseph Daly. There is no immediate reason why you should. A soldier dead for seventy-eight years, he is just one of the British soldiers who have been shot and killed this century. He is a tiny footnote in British imperial history, of interest to a small group of military historians. But for me his life and death illustrate a much bigger story, one that goes to the heart of a very complicated relationship.

But I will come to all that later. First the simple facts of James Daly's life. A native of County Westmeath, in what was then British-ruled Ireland, Daly was a private in the Connaught Rangers, a regiment that has served in the British army since the 1700s. Joining the British army for the proverbial 'shilling a day' was the escape route from poverty for tens of thousands of Irishmen down the years. They fought in every corner of the empire, subduing the natives and imposing the Pax Britannica.

The courage of the Irishmen who fought for Britain in the First and Second World Wars was largely ignored at home. It didn't fit with the prevailing nationalist view of the past. Indeed it took until last November's Remembrance Services before we saw the Queen and the Irish President, Mary McAleese, pay tribute to their memory at Messines Ridge. It was, we were told, an occasion in which the Irish dead were honoured by the people of Ireland. Three-quarters of a century on, we finally reach a point where the

Irish state feels able to commemorate Irishmen who died fighting for Britain.

We have always suffered from a convenient amnesia about Irishmen fighting on the side of the old enemy. I remember a neighbour in Dublin once telling me how her father, who had served at the Somme, had been shunned by local nationalists when he came home from the war. Others became targets and were shot by the IRA. But the simple fact is that the British shilling was all that saved thousands of families from starvation in the tenements of Dublin and the poverty-stricken lands west of the River Shannon. Tradition also had a big role to play. My neighbour's grandfather had served in the Boer war; she still keeps a brush he used for cleaning his uniform. In fact the tradition of southern Irishmen serving in British regiments continues to this day, though not anywhere like on the same scale as before independence.

But back to Private Daly. At the end of June 1920, Daly and the rest of his battalion were stationed at Jullundur, near Amritsar, in British India. The infamous massacre by British troops had taken place only a short time before. The area was seething with nationalist anger, and the soldiers of the Connaught Rangers were an important part of the British garrison. There is little indication of what Daly and his colleagues thought about the massacre. But it would appear they were more concerned with events at home in Ireland. The previous year IRA men had ambushed a group of policemen at Soloheadbeg in County Tipperary. The killings signalled the start of a new, bitter phase in the Irish Troubles.

Within a few months the IRA was launching ambushes on British troops and Irish policemen across the country. It is said that one of the Connaught Rangers, home on holiday from India, was attending a football match when he was held up and searched by British troops. The incident shocked him. A British soldier being searched by British soldiers? What he saw was a country that was fast becoming an armed camp, where everybody was expected to take a side. Being a British soldier made him a target for the IRA, yet the British troops in Ireland regarded him as one of the enemy.

As the conflict escalated, reports of atrocities by British forces began to reach the Connaught Rangers' camp at Jullundur. The precise spark for what happened next is still debated by historians. Some suggest it was a series of attacks by the irregular British forces, known as the Black and Tans, which infuriated Daly and his friends. Others believe it was a massacre by regular troops in Dublin which precipitated the crisis. At this point let me add a personal note: if anybody has further information on the mutiny, anything that illuminates the facts or counters misapprehensions, please get in touch with me.

Whatever the exact incident, Private Daly and up to 150 other men staged a mutiny. It appears to have been a fairly badly organized affair, beginning at Jullundur, then spreading to the mountains. A green flag was raised and the mutineers named their HQ 'Liberty Hall', after the headquarters of James Connolly's Irish Citizen Army that rebelled against the British in 1916. The army chaplain, Father Baker, was the first officer to recognize the inherent danger in the mutiny: should it succeed, the local Indian population would surely be emboldened to strike out at the British. This would give the British a powerful reason to deal ruthlessly with the mutineers. The priest moved quickly to try and defuse the situation. He persuaded Daly and the others to hand in their weapons on the promise that all would be forgotten.

For a while this appeared to work. But tensions rose again. Some say Daly was pressurized by his colleagues, fearful that without weapons they were now at the mercy of the officers. Another theory is that the promise to 'forget about everything' had been broken by the officers. Daly and about forty men drew bayonets and advanced on the arsenal where the weapons were stored. On the way they were confronted by British officers who opened fire. Three men were hit. Two died quickly from their wounds, another died later in hospital from fever. At least two of the dead may have been simply returning from their mess when they wandered accidentally into the line of fire. But the gunfire ended the mutiny. Daly and his followers surrendered and were led away to the notorious prison at Lucknow. It was there, on 2 November 1920, after being court-martialled, that Private James Joseph Daly, accused of being the ring-leader, was led out for execution by firing squad – the last man in the British army to be shot for mutiny. Eighteen others were given the death penalty but had their sentences commuted to life imprisonment. Two years later they were freed when an independent Irish state was declared.

It is in the nature of war to throw up impossible choices. The death of normality that attends the outbreak of war propels men and women into a moral quagmire. To kill or not to kill, to fight or to run, to follow orders or to refuse . . . sooner or later most troops in battle confront these issues. And yet military doctrine, of necessity, demands absolute obedience. That is how armies work. Soldiers are trained to react instinctively to the shouted command. When mutinies happen, they are for the most part the result of soldiers' anger, poor leadership, bad conditions and heavy losses. What happened with Private Daly was different. His choice, and that of the men who supported him, went to the core of his identity. An Irishman in a British uniform, he was still a British citizen. In legal terms he owed his loyalty to the king. But his heart told him otherwise. It is a choice few soldiers ever have to make.

Legally he was wrong. In human terms, though, can we condemn him? I don't believe we should. He and the other mutineers may be a footnote in history. There is no pressure from any source to reappraise the mutiny. But I think that it's high time the British army did. It is time to pardon Private Daly.

THE BOYS OF SUMMER

Belfast, July 1998

In 1969, Belfast's Catholic Ardoyne area was caught up in sectarian violence. Few households were untouched by it. For the youngsters in the district, like those in the Holy Cross football team, sport had to take second place to survival.

As Joe Skelly remembers, it was a hot afternoon in early summer. The boys in the Holy Cross intermediate Gaelic team were about to tog out for the game when Mr Grogan called them over. Pat Grogan was their teacher and coach, a strong man with a quick sense of humour. The boys liked him. He made them feel like winners, not a bunch of awkward eleven-year-olds. That afternoon they'd seen him hauling a large blue bag to the edge of the football field. The boys were dressed in their usual exotic mix of jerseys, most of them hand-me-downs from older brothers, a frayed collage of different colours and sizes. A proper team kit was out of the question. In the Ardoyne of the late sixties unemployment was endemic. The boys' families had more to worry about than football kits.

'Where do you think you lot are goin'?' asked Grogan. 'We're goin' to play the match, sir,' one of them replied. Grogan told them to stand where they were. He opened the big blue bag and reached inside. He began to pull out some football shirts. They were black and white, the colours of Holy Cross Primary School. Grogan handed the jerseys to the astonished youngsters. 'Well yez can't play without a proper kit. Ye can't be winners if ye don't look the part,' he said. Thirty years later, sitting in the front room of his terraced house in Ardoyne, Joe Skelly's face lights up when he describes the moment.

'We all looked at each other. You know we were amazed. It was like putting an international shirt on your back. It was absolutely fantastic. We thought we were going to be the superstars of tomorrow, like we really had it in us to be winners. The teacher told us we had it in us.' Grogan lined the boys up for a photograph in their new kit. For many it was their first experience of standing in front of a camera.

Three decades on we see them staring earnestly at the camera, mindful of their teacher's exhortation to look like winners and not a gang of giddy boys. It is May 1968. The world is in turmoil: '68 is the year of revolution and murder, the time of the street-fighting man. There are riots on the streets of Paris and Chicago, Robert Kennedy and Martin Luther King are murdered in the United States, the Prague Spring is crushed. Closer to home there will be stirrings as Ulster's Catholics begin to agitate for civil rights. After forty years of discrimination and exclusion the Catholics want a fair share of jobs and houses, an end to the gerrymandering of local government, and reform of the police. But the boys of Holy Cross Primary are untouched.

Later that year they will repay Pat Grogan's investment of time, money and hope by winning the Belfast Intermediate League. Winners! There was a cup. There were medals. The school went wild with excitement. The players were hailed as local heroes. 'We were the boys that summer all right, we were the boys,' says Joe Skelly. He remembers a team of fairly mixed talent. There were a few real stars like Seamus Clarke and big Ciaran Murphy and Maurice Gilvarry. Tough boys on the field but relaxed and easy-going once the final whistle went.

Ciaran's older brother Pat was one of the best players in the district, an all-rounder who excelled at Gaelic football and soccer. He and Ciaran were inseparable. As Pat remembers, they were more best friends than brothers. Being the older of the two Pat was detailed to take care of his younger brother. Growing up in the two-bedroomed terraced house, they had shared the same bed. When Pat produces the family photograph album, you notice that he is never pictured without his smaller brother. The two boys dressed as cowboys. The two of them playing in the yard. There is a sense of ease and real affection in these images. None of the usual sibling rivalry. 'He was an original, you know, a big lump of a lad,' recalls Pat.

The Murphys lived near and knew the Gilvarry family. With twelve thousand people crammed into an area of barely half a square mile chances are everybody will know everybody else. Pat remembers Maurice Gilvarry as a very quiet individual. He was a bit of a loner, he says. There were eleven Gilvarrys, crammed into a two-bedroomed house. This was not untypical of Catholic families of the period. Ask Eamon Gilvarry about his brother and the football team and he smiles. Eamon played for the team as well but was never good enough to make the final side. His brother Maurice, he says, was skilful but shortsighted. He was good around the field but could be disastrous near the goal. Once during a crucial game Eamon saw Maurice standing directly in front of the goal with the keeper at his mercy. Maurice swung at the ball but missed completely, his leg slashing vainly at the air. 'I remember we were all shouting at him and slagging him and keeping him going. The goal was wide open but he never touched the ball. God it was funny.'

But the days of laughter were to disappear in the spring and summer of 1969. The boys still trained and played. Pat Grogan urged them on to greater glory. But as the civil rights agitation continued, sectarian tension escalated. Going to and from football training was becoming a hazardous business. The problem for the team was that Ardoyne was largely surrounded by Loyalist territory. To the west the Shankill Road, to the north and east were the Upper Crumlin Road and Ballysillan. The pitch the boys used for training was smack in the heart of Ballysillan. Sectarian name-calling and skirmishing with the Protestants became a regular occurrence. And then in August '69 the balloon went up.

Ulster exploded into communal violence with Protestant mobs

laying siege to Catholic ghettos in Belfast. There were pitched battles in Derry with the RUC and B-Specials on one side and Catholic youths on the other. Ardoyne came under attack with rows of houses burned down and hundreds of people forced to flee the district. For Eamon Gilvarry it began with the sound of crowds running down the street outside the window of the bedroom he shared with Maurice. 'You just never slept. I mean you knew what was going on outside. There was a lot of shooting and I remember the taste of the CS gas. It didn't sink in, though, until you read the paper. I remember seeing that on the fourteenth or fifteenth of August a man sitting in his house here had been shot by the police. That's when it hit you, when you knew how serious it was.'

The neighbourhood organized its own defence. Buses were hijacked and placed across the narrow streets. Maurice and Eamon Gilvarry, Pat and Ciaran Murphy, Joe Skelly and Seamus Clarke – all joined in the rioting. Pat Murphy says that in the beginning they were all naive. They were caught up in the excitement and fear. Football had been overtaken by the more pressing need to defend the neighbourhood. One of his strongest memories is of watching a group of young men running across waste ground while snipers were firing at them. The fleeing group were holding a piece of corrugated tin over their heads – a shield that would provide no protection if the snipers managed to find their range. Luckily the gunmen were bad shots. 'It shows how naive we were about firearms and what they could do to you,' he says.

Sooner or later the war visited a personal agony on most homes in the district. It could be a death, an injury, an arrest. Some of the football team moved away with their families. Others like the Skellys and Clarkes and Gilvarrys stayed. For a short time Ciaran Murphy and his mother emigrated to America. But the call of home proved too strong and they returned. It was a fateful move. Pat Murphy still struggles with the memory of what happened to Ciaran. One night in 1974 the big footballer was walking home along Cliftonville Road, about ten minutes from his home, when a car pulled up alongside. There was a struggle and Ciaran was dragged inside. The facts, barely adequate to describe the horror, come from police records: a young Catholic male stabbed repeatedly, shot several times in the face and body. The same body which had run on fields of glory with Holy Cross was found in a bloody heap on the mountains overlooking Ardoyne. A random victim in a time full of random victims. The team's trainer Pat Grogan was another, shot dead at his home by the UVF.

The nature of the conflict changed over the years. The army came in. The IRA reappeared. Riots gave way to gun battles. Bombs were exploding all over the city. To the British army and police Ardoyne was IRA territory. It was a place where soldiers were ambushed and killed. There were raids in the middle of the night. Doors kicked in, men dragged from their beds. Bitterness was deepening. A soft-spoken teacher from County Limerick, Tom Dore remembers giving religious instruction classes to the boys from Holy Cross while the streets outside erupted in violence. 'They were young fellows on the threshold of life and had they been brought up anywhere else they would have gotten jobs or gone on to university. But what happened was that their whole lives were restricted. They couldn't travel outside their own area. They had to survive. I tried to preach the gospel of forgiveness but I often felt I was getting nowhere.'

Tom has particularly fond memories of one member of the team, Seamus Clarke. 'He was a fantastic fellow. If I had bet on anything it would have been that he might have become a bishop or something.' Instead Seamus became a leading IRA man and is now living in the Irish Republic. He is still wanted in Northern Ireland to complete a sentence for terrorist offences. Seamus Clarke wasn't the only member of the team to join the IRA. Some time in the mid to late seventies Maurice Gilvarry also joined up. He had been picked up by the army during the sweeps that came with internment in 1974 and deposited in Long Kesh. At the age of sixteen he was one of the youngest internees. After his release

Maurice became an active member of the Belfast IRA. Eamon Gilvarry remembers his brother seeming a great deal older when he came out of Long Kesh. He no longer wanted to play football. 'In the beginning, around '68/69, we didn't know who was in the IRA. Who are the IRA, who the hell are they, we used to ask and we'd never have known until all this blew up. Why did Maurice join up? To follow his mates? I never asked . . .'

In fact Eamon knew nothing of his brother's secret life. And then one weekend in the winter of 1981 Maurice went missing. Eamon spent the weekend going around the pubs and clubs of Ardoyne trying to track him down, without success. And then on the following Tuesday he switched on the lunch-time news to hear that a body had been found on the border with the Irish Republic. The man had been shot in the head and was found with his hands tied behind his back. It was Maurice. The IRA issued a statement saying he had been executed as an informer. Eamon's most painful memory is of the funeral. As the coffin was being carried up through Ardoyne he noticed a group of local Republicans standing on the corner. They were laughing, deliberately and ostentatiously. 'Them three boys stood there and laughed. They laughed as we passed them with the coffin. I never laughed at anybody's death.'

And that is where the story of the boys of Holy Cross might end. Loss and grief and a certain amount of bitterness. But there is a postscript of hope. In the summer of 1998 – thirty years after the photograph was taken – there is peace in Ardoyne. The rioting and gun battles are over. The Good Friday Agreement has been signed. Children are playing on the streets outside new houses. Eamon Gilvarry tells me the peace is the best chance for a generation, that he feels hope in spite of his anger. And a few streets away, on the Gaelic football pitch, Pat Murphy is shouting instructions to a group of youngsters. They are the Holy Cross team of 1998 and Pat is telling them they can be winners if they make the effort. It is up to them, he says. Up to them.

Part Four

FROM A DRIFTING CONTINENT

AU REVOIR, MES ENFANTS

Butare/London, March/April 1999

Five years after the genocide in Rwanda, which cost the lives of up to a million people, normality was beginning to return to everyday life. But memories of the slaughter remained fresh and many of those responsible for the killing had not been brought to justice.

This is not the town I remember. There are no road blocks. No militiamen. The guesthouse we stayed in has become a Red Cross centre. At night we used to sit next to those windows and listen to the militiamen getting drunk at the road blocks. Now the sounds are very different. The difference between the sound of life and the sound of death. I hear African laughter and the jangle of Zairean guitar music. This, I tell myself, is entirely logical. But I am momentarily caught in a time warp. My memory spills over and floods the present. Where are the killers? Where are the machetes? What has happened to that smell of dead people? Butare is a changed town. Outside the prefet's office where the frightened Tutsis went for shelter (I can still see their eyes, reproaching me, I who went away when the army pointed their guns and told me to leave) there is now only neatly cut grass.

It is late afternoon and a beautiful honey-coloured light is flooding down the main street. In the cathedral – vast, gothic and wholly out of place – they are celebrating Palm Sunday. The voices of nuns singing an Ave float across but I want to hear that Zairean pop. Tomorrow I will be meeting the nuns, I will be asking them questions and reviving bad memories. And so, if you please, let me just hide in this wild music from over the border . . .

Families pass down the street making their way to the cathedral and carrying bundles of palms. A crowd of people are sitting drinking beer outside the Hotel Ibis. Their laughter is sprinkled in the air around me. The Hotel Ibis is where I will sleep tonight and where, five years ago, the militia leader Robert Kajuga held sway with his retinue. By the time he arrived in Butare, Kajuga and his men had killed several hundred thousand Tutsis. They brought with them Tutsi women, kept women, safe while they gave their bodies to the killers. What became of those girls when Kajuga and the others were driven out of Rwanda? Did they survive? I heard later that he had died of Aids in Congo Brazzaville. Kajuga, whom everybody said was a Tutsi himself, but who rose to become the most powerful of the Hutu extremist leaders. So great was the fear Kajuga inspired that his Tutsi women could wander into the market without being immediately set upon and killed.

Today there are plenty of soldiers around. But these are Tutsis, the new masters of Rwanda. There are no militiamen and no machetes and no blood. And something else that is new: there are lots of street children, ragged and persistent, who swarm around you on the street, pulling at your clothes and demanding money until a man runs out of the hotel and kicks one of them. The boy screams and runs away.

Suddenly I remember a scene from five years ago: we had crossed the border near Butare and gone into Burundi. At the first big town we stopped to buy beers. The town was full of Rwandan refugees. We noticed a big commotion in the middle of the market. I walked across and a group of men were beating the hell out of a small boy. This was very heavy stuff. They were hammering him – leather belts, sticks and anything else they could lay their hands on. I was sure they were going to kill him. And so I stepped in. I tried to intervene. The men suddenly stopped their attack. In that flash of a second the boy scuttled between their legs and ran away. Furious, the men turned on me. They began to push and jostle, screaming all the while. My producer Rizu had grown up in Tanzania and knew the score: thieves got killed by mobs all the time. And by stepping in to help the kid I had interposed myself between the criminal and justice. She pushed me towards the car and tried to calm the crowd. Speaking in Swahili she placated them. I was a foreigner. I did not understand. Thank you, thank you, thank you, she said. And it worked and I am forever thankful to Rizu.

The street boys of Butare are more aggressive than any street children I've ever met.

Somebody says they are Hutu kids who were separated from their parents in the great journey back from the camps in Zaire and Burundi. I try to picture what they will have seen and what they have lost. There will be no future for them here. To be Hutu in this new Rwanda is hard enough. To be a Hutu street kid . . . there is no place further for you to fall in terms of social standing.

The new Tutsi elite occupy the verandah of the Ibis Hotel. They are mostly Tutsi businessmen. There are some aid workers here too, and – bizarre to my eyes – a party of elderly Americans who are on a tour of Central Africa. One of them tells me they are from a Christian Fellowship and have come to spread the gospel of love. Everybody has been so friendly, she says, so receptive to the message. All that hatred is a thing of the past, she assures me.

On the television in the main bar there are scenes of terror from Kosovo, long lines of refugees crossing into Albania on their little red tractors. This is late March, at the beginning of the Serbian terror in Kosovo. But none of the drinkers pays much attention. Down here they've seen all that and a lot worse. Five years ago the Hutu extremists raised the bar for everyone in the atrocity stakes: a million dead and an entire population displaced. The Tutsis and the aid workers and the Americans keep eating and drinking and soon somebody switches to the sports channel.

My translator's name is Michael. He knows Butare very well. I should say that he knows a particular roofspace in a particular house very well. It was here that he spent three months hiding out from the Hutu extremists as they combed the town for Tutsis. He was hidden by a Hutu who had been a friend of his father, a man of courage who risked his own life providing shelter to one of the 'cockroaches'. Michael is tall and gentle and he is having a hard time of it on this trip. We are hearing too many stories of what happened five years ago. And Michael has too many stories of his own. Enough to fill a book, he says. 'When this is over I am going to write a book about it,' he tells me. 'But it is over, the genocide is over,' I reply. At this he looks at me and smiles. What is his expression? Weariness? Contempt?

Michael is alive but his parents and God knows how many members of his extended family are dead. He took us to his parents' house the other night. It must have been a beautiful spot before the militia got there. Very modern and split-level with a long garden, sitting in the hills beyond Kigali. The bush has taken over now. There are thick vines growing down through the spiral staircase, weeds and wild flowers have colonized the driveway and the grass in the garden is nearly waist high. Michael points to the stairs and says his parents were killed upstairs and then dragged down to ground level to be set on fire.

The bodies were partially burned. When Michael eventually emerged from hiding he and his brothers went home. And after the horror and the shock they buried their parents' bodies in the garden.

As we drank our beers in the Ibis, Michael reminded me that five years ago the Tutsis here would have been dragged out on to the street and hacked to death. And I, who have not returned since the great slaughter, am still finding it hard to get a grasp on what I am seeing here in Butare. Tutsis. Tutsis eating. Drinking. Walking around. Doing business. Tutsis alive. My friends have told me I am unhealthily obsessed with this country. It is time to leave all that behind, one of them said before I left. But leave what behind? You cannot say goodbye to memory. It is a diligent, determined companion.

You go away, immerse yourself in other stories and places. But Rwanda does not go away. The nightmares are long gone. They aren't the problem. It is the stuff that comes up when you are awake. The endless question: 'Why?' Perhaps I am looking for a kind of spiritual understanding here. I don't believe in the 'heart of darkness' bullshit peddled by the popular press. But there are questions beyond the historical, the strictly factual, that I want to ask. Tomorrow I will meet a nun and hear her story. A woman of God who survived the evil and who is burdened by some private darkness. People told me she was haunted by questions. Something had happened in front of her eyes which she could not mitigate with the assurance of faith.

That night in my bedroom in the Ibis Hotel I listen to one of those great Rwandan rainstorms and afterwards the chorus of the tree frogs and crickets. They reach a crescendo just before dawn, a sound from a million years ago, full of swamp and fecundity. It is the sound of the world beginning. Did the hiding and the hunted hear that sound every morning? They must have. What did they think of that life bursting into the air around them? Most of those who hid were eventually found and hacked to death. I have been awake all night. My first night back and I am spooked beyond words. I turn over in bed and think about 1994, again. The room is big – you could have had ten or more men quartered here. I start to wonder who slept in this room back then, after which crimes. Who lay in my bed? Did he take care to wash the blood from his hands? Or did he fall drunk and exhausted into sleep? There are, as I say, so many questions.

The nun works in the hospital. Drive out of town in the direction of Kigali and up a ridge and you come to the Butare University Hospital. We spend the best part of a day trying to find the nun. Her Reverend Mother says we can speak to her whenever we like. But getting a face-to-face meeting with Sister Speciose Mukarabayiza turns out to be the problem. She always seems to have just left the place we've arrived at. Smiling nuns point us on our way. They are very helpful, though I wonder if Sister Speciose would rather not be found. But eventually messages get through and connections are made. We meet her after mass in a room at the hospital.

The hospital is where the militia and the army killed around three thousand people. They worked their way through the crowds in the usual way. Chop, shoot, club, hack. It cannot have been too hard a job. Many of the dead were injured or sick to begin with. They weren't going to be running anywhere. If you walk behind the hospital you notice a wide field which is used as a dump. There are pieces of builders' rubble and various bits of used medical kit – syringes, facemasks, empty pill bottles. And if you look carefully you will see pieces of human bone. A femur, a piece of a skull. They are left over from the genocide. Whoever was given the job of re-burying the dead after the slaughter must have missed these.

By African standards it is a nice modern hospital. It would not look out of place in most European countries. That, by the way, is one of the scary things about Rwanda. You are not talking primitive backwater here. The killing was done in fine handsome churches, in neat and orderly local authority buildings, on roads that were among the best on the continent, and in clean modern hospitals like this.

The nun is a gentle, round-faced woman whose speaking voice is close to a whisper. She is a Tutsi and a member of the Benebikira sisters. But she does not have what might be called a 'classical' Tutsi appearance. She is short and plump and might easily pass for a Hutu. We go to a room away from the main hospital complex. It is quiet in here and I don't have to strain to hear what she is saying. Michael tells her of his time in Butare, the months hiding in the attic and the never-ending fear of discovery. And the nun nods because she knows all about this. That is the point of my visit. Her knowledge, her helplessness, her defeat.

It started in the last week of April, 1994. Up to then Butare had escaped the horror which had swept the rest of the country. The local prefet, Jean Habyalimana was a Tutsi and worked hard, travelling from commune to commune to preach a message of peace and tolerance. But with the government now in the hands of an extremist clique Habyalimana's days were numbered. And then the hardliners took over. The government leaders came to town and Habyalimana was fired. They held a big meeting and announced there and then that he was finished. After hiding out for a while he was arrested and executed. His wife and children were wiped out too. A new prefet, Sylvain Nsabimana, was appointed and a new army commander, Lt Colonel Tharcisse Muvunyi, arrived in town. The massacres began in Butare shortly afterwards.

They may have started later than the rest of the country but the killers of Butare quickly caught up. No Tutsi was to be left alive here. They killed in all the usual ways but also managed to be brutally inventive. One of their execution methods was to force their victims to dig deep trenches which would be filled with gasoline and set alight. The Tutsis were forced to jump into the inferno.

Professor Pierre Karenzi would have seen all of this. But perhaps he believed his status as Rwanda's foremost scientist – he was a physicist – would protect him. Several of his colleagues from the staff of the university were members of the new ruling clique in Butare – Hutu extremists, yes, but old colleagues all the same. One morning Professor Karenzi walked down the main street and ran straight into an army road block. The men at the barrier were members of the Presidential Guard, the principal masters of terror in Butare. But standing further up the road was Jean Birchmans Nyshamuriya, vice-rector of the university. Karenzi would have seen him there and perhaps assumed that with such a leading member of the clique nearby, an old colleague, he would be safe. But Karenzi was grabbed by the soldiers and shot dead. Bang, bang. Dead in the flicker of an eyelid. And Birchmans did nothing. Why should he have? Karenzi was a Tutsi and Birchmans had dedicated months to preparing his people for war against these cockroaches. Set against the imperative of extermination a long-standing professional relationship meant nothing.

Some time later the army and militia went to Karenzi's house and murdered his wife. The professor's children and some friends staying with them had been hidden in the roof. Mrs Karenzi had a strong sense that she would not survive the slaughter and so she gave the children precise instructions about what they should do if she were killed. They were to make their way to the convent of the Benebikira sisters in the centre of Butare. The children heard their mother being killed. When the noise died away and they were sure the militia had gone, the children came out of their hiding place. They dragged their mother's body inside the house to prevent it being eaten by the packs of dogs which were now running wild across the countryside. And then they set out to try and reach the convent. There were ten of them.

Mrs Speciose Kanyabugoyi lives in a big empty house in the hills above Kigali. You reach it by driving along a rutted lane. In the rainy season the track turns to mush and you slide around, struggling to keep the car out of the storm drain on the side of the track. Mrs Kanyabugoyi welcomes us with a tray of lemonade. A tall and striking woman she is anxious to tell her story. But hers is a house full of long silences.

There are several photographs on the wall. One is of a small boy in a brightly striped shirt playing football. His name is Thierry. His brother Emery is on the other wall. He looks at the camera with a deeply serious expression. Emery is the younger but the family called him the 'little old man'. He was a kid who worried a lot, who took life very seriously, his mother says. By contrast his older brother Thierry was a happy-go-lucky boy. He was a footballer and liked to joke a lot. When she talks about them Mrs Kanyabugoyi starts to cry. These are children of the past tense. The photographs capture them in that last period of light before the great catastrophe.

On the other side of the room there is a photo-montage. Pictures of young people and old people. Mrs Kanyabugoyi points to the photo of an old man wearing a traditional long robe and standing beside a cow. The old man was her father and like most of the thirty-odd people in the frame he was killed in the genocide. I ask about her husband. Dead too. So are most of her brothers and sisters and her Tutsi neighbours. How did she survive?

Mrs Kanyabugoyi tells me that she went to the Ecole Technique – a big modern school – with several thousand other Tutsis soon after the killing started. They were protected by Belgian troops from the small United Nations force in Rwanda. All day they could see the militia driving around outside, waiting for a chance to attack. But the Belgians kept them at bay. And then one day the Belgians decided to leave. They were ordered to go by their commanders. People screamed and begged. They knew they were being left to die. The Belgians pushed them back as they retreated on to their trucks. The militia could see all of this. They barely waited for the Belgians to drive out one exit before they entered through another gate. And then they killed and pillaged. Mrs Kanyabugoyi's husband was murdered. She survived by lying among the bodies and feigning death.

Although she is traumatized by the memory, I sense that this is the easier part of the story to tell. It is the matter of her two boys which renders her distraught. We sit down and she begins to talk.

In the weeks leading up to the genocide she and her husband could sense something bad was going to happen. She was a human rights activist and kept a close tab on the disappearances and killings which were happening around the country. And like every other Rwandan, like all the foreign diplomats and UN soldiers, she could see the militia training on the streets. Frightened for her boys she made the decision to take them out of Kigali, to head for Butare where the family friend Professor Karenzi had offered to take care of them until things blew over. That was how many saw it then. There would be trouble but – as had often happened in the past – it would eventually blow over. Rwanda's Tutsis were used to purges. People got killed or thrown in jail. And then after the point had been made, the situation returned to 'normal'.

Butare was seen as a more civilized place. The university town of Rwanda. A place of churches and convents and seminaries. And besides it was a short trip across the border to Burundi if things went wrong. Mrs Kanyabugoyi took her sons to the home of the

Karenzi family. There were other children for them to play with and, she noticed, the atmosphere in Butare was much calmer than in the capital.

And now as she speaks her voice begins to falter and tears come to her eyes.

'When I was leaving, the older boy looked at me with tears in his eyes. It was as if he knew something was going to happen, that we would not see each other again. And I felt so guilty leaving them. But I had no choice. I wanted them out of Kigali, in a safer place,' she says.

The room is quiet. Mrs Kanyabugoyi twists the wedding ring on her finger. I am looking at her, imagining that long journey back to Kigali and her wondering, wondering what the boys were thinking and feeling, her wondering what would happen to them all.

They arrived at the convent in the evening. There were a few tentative knocks on the gate. The nun remembered that the sun was glowing bright orange that night. In that strange, lovely light the children appeared. Some of them were naked, most of them in rags. 'They looked so frightened. I have never seen anything like the expressions on their faces. So much fear,' she said. They had been attacked by soldiers but another group, apparently tired of killing, decided to intervene and spare their lives. They were taken to the convent, a little band of survivors asking for sanctuary. They ranged in age from a little girl of seven to a woman of twenty-two. She was Solange Karenzi, the daughter of the professor, and a very beautiful young woman. And with her, Thierry and Emery.

The nuns brought them in. They washed them and clothed them. They gave them food and then sat and prayed with them. And then they found hiding places in the convent. Some went into the ceiling, others into cupboards and wardrobes. Into every secret place in the convent children crept and hid. They would come down at night, said Sister Speciose; they would come down to eat and use the toilet and to talk. And they prayed a great deal. 'Once they asked me if they would survive and I said that God was good and that yes, they would survive.' The nun suspects the children did not believe her.

The killers were still active on the streets outside. There was much shooting and there were explosions and cries of pain. The death toll in Butare would soon reach three hundred thousand. Almost all of them Tutsis, all unarmed innocent civilians. The nuns knew they were taking a huge risk in sheltering the children. For Sister Speciose it was a double risk. As a Tutsi she was herself lucky to be alive. Her holy orders would be of little use if she were caught sheltering these little cockroaches. The nuns debated about what to do. Keeping the children in the convent ran the risk of a raid and everybody being killed. But it was impossible to try and smuggle them out. The militia were everywhere. The road down to the Burundi border had more than twenty road blocks. And the border itself was notoriously dangerous. People had been hacked and shot trying to run across the bridge into Burundi. And so they waited and prayed.

On the morning of 30 April there were loud bangs on the convent gate. Outside, the nuns could see militiamen and soldiers. Among them was Lieutenant Ildephonse Hategekimana. He told the nuns he had a search warrant signed by the local military commander, Lt Colonel Tharcisse Muvunyi. The Lieutenant showed the warrant and then told his men to search. The children were either discovered or came voluntarily out of their hiding places when called, as if they knew the end had come and that resistance was futile. They were lined up in the garden among the flowers. The nuns tried to argue but could do nothing.

As Sister Speciose is telling me this she looks at the ground and shakes her head. 'The Tutsi children said nothing at all. They just stood there looking so frightened.' It was their Hutu friends – children who were also staying at the convent – who began to cry.

There were twenty-five people in all whom the soldiers decided to remove, most of them were children. The youngest was a little girl called Aimee who was just five years old. They were marched out through the gates and put on a truck. As the nuns watched, the soldiers climbed aboard and stood on top of the children. The memory of this is too much for the nun and she stops speaking.

They brought you out and pushed you on to the lorry. Some of them were drunk. The militia were circling around, anxious to get on with the job. Thierry and Eric. The smiling footballer and the worried little boy. Your mother had brought you here for safety. Butare. A civilized town. Now in front of the cathedral the soldiers and militia shouted at you and jostled. And the soldiers made you lie down and they stood on top of you. Fully grown men stamping on your small bones. Did you know then that it was coming to an end? Or did you believe it when they said you were being taken to the prefet's office for safe keeping? Maybe you clung to some kind of hope.

But I suspect it vanished by the time you reached the forest. That was where we think they took you off the lorries, where they pushed you down on to the ground and began their work. A five-year-old is quick. Not that many blows of a machete or a club to kill little Aimee. One or two at the most. It would have taken longer with the older children, unless they used bullets. But we have no way of knowing. All we know is that you vanished into the forest and that you are buried in one of the mass graves.

The good nun who cared for you is tormented now. Not a day goes by, she says, that your faces do not return to her. She blames herself for not dying as well. She wants me to understand that it was a time of madness, that there was nothing she could have done. I know that it was, I was there for some of it myself. But no words of mine can ease that pain or answer her questions. Why should the innocent feel guilt?

I will tell you the story of my own few days in Butare. We drove up from Burundi, through all those road blocks with their wild-eyed drunken peasants dangling grenades and waving machetes. I will tell you how sick with fear I was. Me a foreigner, an outsider, a member of no targeted group. I was shaking with the terror of it. And I, dear sister, knew I would be getting out in a few days.

In the town there were killers everywhere. Most of the Tutsis were dead by then, but there was a group outside the prefet's office. They were ragged and hungry and terrified. The prefet, Sylvain Nsabimana, told us they would be safe from harm while they remained there. But we knew that gangs were coming at night and dragging some of them away. The prefet seemed a reasonable man but I hear now that he is on trial for genocide. The evidence suggests he was a much more dangerous person than I ever imagined.

On our last night we went back to try and see the Tutsis. But they were under military guard and the soldiers came down and forced us away. And I did not stay, sister. I did not try to get past them or mount a vigil. I was frightened, sister, more frightened than I have ever been in my life. I got into our car and drove away, sister.

There are killers and there are masters of killing. There are blood-thirsty monsters and men who fail the test of civilized behaviour through weakness or moral blindness. I believe that Lt Colonel Tharcisse Muvunyi belongs in the latter category. Muvunyi was the military commander of the Butare area during the worst of the genocide. He did not exercise control over all the troops or the militiamen. The presidential guard behaved pretty much as it wanted to. But Muvunyi was a central figure. As a senior army commander he was loyal to the genocidal government and eyewitnesses say he was among those who incited villagers to murder on at least one occasion. He knew what his soldiers were doing. According to the report of the respected group Human Rights Watch the genocide was highly successful in Butare thanks to the muscular assistance of the military. The organization also says that Muvunyi signed the warrant which led to the arrest and murder of the children at Benebikira.

Throughout the slaughter Muvunyi remained a senior officer of the Rwandan army. The Rwandan government believes he was a central figure in the planning of the genocide. There are, it should be said, those who say Muvunyi helped a number of Tutsis to escape from Butare. Personal friends, people for whom he may have felt sympathy in one way or another. It is also true that some in the Presidential Guard did not believe he was a true extremist.

But the inescapable fact is that he was one of the top military officers in the country. And he must bear responsibility for the crimes of the men he allowed loose in the community. Not once did he speak out against the genocide, nor did he attempt to leave Rwanda and seek asylum abroad. Had he been truly opposed to the genocide he would hardly have remained in the bloodstained ranks of the FAR (Forces Armée Rwandaise). The fact is that Muvunyi stayed with the project to the bitter end when the Hutu extremists were driven out of Rwanda. I don't believe he was an idealogue, rather an opportunist who liked his position of power and who lacked the courage to pull back from evil.

London

The woman in the flat is uncomfortable. She knows she has made a big mistake just letting us in. But she is instinctually polite and, I suspect, a little intimidated by us. She lives here with her two daughters. They arrived from Zambia last year as asylum seekers. It is strange to hear them speaking Kinyarwanda here in a council flat in South London. We talk about Rwanda. I discover that her husband was the former minister of Public Works. He was a known extremist (she does not say this, of course) and fled to Zambia after the genocide. He died there of Aids last year. She gestures at the tiny sitting room, at the grotty couch and tells me about the wonderful house she once had in Rwanda.

I try her on the subject of Muvunyi. She says that she knows the family but they don't meet that often. And then she lets slip that he lives in Lewisham. Could she give me the exact address, I wonder? It's just that there are all these stories going around about the colonel and I would like to ask him some questions. She picks up the phone and telephones the Muvunyis. A woman at the other end wants to know who we are and what we want. There is a short explanation and then the conversation ends. 'She promises she will call back,' our host says. We wait. Another half hour passes in pointless conversation. There is no return call. And so we keep talking. In ten minutes we manage to extract Muvunyi's telephone number. As she is giving us the number my colleague Ian manages to read the address upside down from the little book the woman is holding. We learn that Muvunyi is studying English, that he has done some charitable work helping Rwandan refugees in London (Hutus it goes without saying).

We leave and head straight away to a long suburban avenue about a mile away. On the way we talk about the Benebikira children. If I am to confront Muvunyi I need to remember them, to make myself understand why I am about to knock on this door and shatter a man's peace.

As it happens, he is not in. His daughter comes to the door and takes a message. Later he telephones me. 'This is Tharcisse,' says the voice. His English is very good. But he will not give an interview, he will not respond to any questions. That is the advice of his lawyer. Call back next week, he says. And I do call back again and again. But the colonel will not talk.

We go back to the avenue in South London. It is six-thirty in the morning and people are just beginning to get up and go out to work. We wait and wait. There is no sign. Suddenly there is movement at the door. Two teenage boys – the Muvunyi twins – leave and walk up the street to school. An hour later a woman comes out and walks away. But there is no sign of Muvunyi himself. At one o'clock we decide to give it fifteen more minutes. And then ten minutes after the hour the door of the Muvunyi flat opens and a woman walks out. She must be his wife. She looks to be in her late forties or early fifties. She checks the street carefully, looking up and down. But she does not see us sitting in the car. And then a man steps out. He is slim and tall. He is wearing a black leather jacket and blue jeans. The man smiles at the woman and they laugh at whatever it is he has said. They move down the street towards us. I see the face and recognize Lt Colonel Tharcisse Muvunyi, Commander of the Butare Military Region, Rwanda, 1994.

We slip out of the car and wait until they have walked past us down the other side of the street. And then we switch on the camera and walk up behind Muvunyi. For a second I feel a twinge of guilt. Here is a man who has walked out of his front door on a sunny day, a man whose kids are in a good school, who is sharing a joke with his wife as they set off for the city to do some shopping. And I am about to come walking out of his past with some of the hardest questions on earth.

The guilt vanishes quickly and I shout out: 'Lt Colonel Muvunyi . . . we would like to talk to you.' He looks around and sees us. 'Oh God, no,' he shouts. And then: 'Go away, go away.' Then he starts to run. I mean really run. Sprinting down the road as fast as he can. Muvunyi is fit. He moves faster than we can. I shout out that I want to talk about crimes against humanity. But the colonel keeps running. Up the steps to the railway station. Along the platform and over the bridge, his wife struggling to catch up and failing. My last sight of him is of a silhouette storming across the bridge and disappearing from view.

We contact the Home Office and they say they don't discuss individual cases. The Rwandan government says it wants to extradite him but knows the British won't send him to a country that has the death penalty. And the International War Crimes Tribunal indicates it won't be chasing him. There are just too many bigger fish on the loose. And so the colonel will live here in Britain until his case comes up for review some time early in the new century. And only he knows whether he is troubled by the events of that mad spring and summer of 1994.

Kigali

To make a genocide you need lots of different kinds of people. The ones who give the orders; the ones who do the killing; the ones who ignore the evidence of their eyes; the powerful countries who could do something but refuse. It took all of these people to make the Rwandan nightmare and we must accept now that most of them will never be punished.

So what is left to the survivors? Mrs Kanyabugoyi wants her children's killers to face trial but knows they probably never will. And she keeps coming back to her own 'failure'. How she was unable to protect the children from the monsters who would do them harm.

In the middle of our interview it becomes clear that Michael, the translator, is unable to continue. His body begins to heave with emotion. He is a survivor and has connected with this in a way I cannot begin to comprehend. He retreats to a corner of the room while we continue the interview in French.

At the end, just before we left her house, Mrs Kanyabugoyi said we should meet some special people. As she opened the back door a group of children trooped in. It was as if they had been lined up and were waiting outside. They were polite and shook hands with each of us. One of them was Mrs Kanyabugoyi's daughter, who survived the genocide. The smallest was a little girl of about three. She was a niece and had been born after the slaughter. When she was old enough Mrs Kanyabugoyi planned to tell her the story of her dead cousins. But that would be some time in the future, when she was old enough to understand.

RETURN TO SOUTH AFRICA

Johannesburg, January 1997

The author, by now the BBC's Asia correspondent resident in Hong Kong, returned to the scene of an earlier posting. He'd been based in South Africa during the violent run-up to the historic all-party elections which swept Nelson Mandela to power. Now he was returning there for a family holiday.

My friend and colleague Allan Little had warned on the phone that I would find a very different country. 'It's a more normal place than the one you left,' he said. At the time of our conversation, I wondered what he really meant. How could it be different? I had left just after the 1994 elections. What could have changed so substantially in that time and what in God's name could have happened to normalize a country like South Africa?

Now, having been back there for several weeks, I think I understand what Allan meant by 'different' and 'normal'. You see, I lived in a country which, all too often, felt like a pressure cooker waiting to blow. My days were spent rushing around burning townships or travelling to far-flung right-wing towns to watch the posturing antics of Eugene Terre'Blanche and his extremist friends. There was enough energy in the air to light up the African continent. It could leave you feeling more exhilarated than you ever thought possible or in the deepest of deep depressions.

When I came to South Africa, at the age of twenty-nine, I was full of the certainty – perhaps even the arrogance – of a young man on his first foreign posting. I was a man with answers and a man in a hurry. But the truth was that I knew very little. Yes, I had been to the country before and I had read all the books and the newspaper cuttings but there are deeper truths about a society that only living there can reveal. And, for me, the search for those truths involved a journey that tested me in ways I could never have imagined. I feel a certain weariness now when I think of those days. It was exciting, yes, but the price was high. Some paid in emotional terms, others with their lives. Among the dead journalists I remember are Keno Stabrook, Abdul Sheriff, Kevin Carter and my own colleague, John Harrison. Good men, dead before their time.

Last week, as we drove around Johannesburg, my wife recalled how she dreaded my daily departures for the townships. The dawn patrols to count the bodies in Katlahong, Soweto, Tokoza, Alexandra. Names engraved for ever into my memory. But oh, there was hope too and laughter and the ultimate triumph of reason. How could I be anything but grateful to have been there on the day of the first non-racial elections when seventy-year-old Robert Captain stood outside the polling booth in Soweto and told me: 'Today I became a human being once more.'

On the road with me always was Milton Nkosi, my friend, guide, interpreter of languages and events. He's still helping to interpret the new South Africa for a new generation of BBC correspondents. Though we couldn't see it at the time, he and I, as much as any of the activists on the streets around us, were riding on a rollercoaster. How alive we felt then. How gripped by the moment, by the passion and clarity and the great sweep of history. There was a camaraderie, a closeness I had never known before and I doubt I'll ever know again. South Africa was less a place, a country, than a love affair. I left it but it never left me. I thought of all this as I drove around Johannesburg and then down through the country to the Cape. The landscape, the great endlessness of veld and mountain that folds and unfolds from the Limpopo to Cape Agulhas, was unchanged. It was springtime, the season of jacaranda and early rains. Now I was travelling with a baby, willing him to share the love of the land which I felt so deeply. But, at ten months, he was naturally more concerned with being fed and petted and escaping from the agonies of his car seat.

Daniel's timely cries ensured I kept my feet on the ground.

Over a seven-week period we drove several thousand kilometres and spoke with countless South Africans, black and white. The old tension and edge had disappeared, replaced by the demands of normal politics for housing, education and economic growth. That's not to say that the past and its miseries don't constantly make their presence felt. The hearings of the Truth and Reconciliation Commission alone ensure this but there is a palpable sense of a new country emerging, in which the political debate is not shaped by the pressures of mass action or communal violence. Increasingly, the cut and thrust of politics is concerned with what Allan Little correctly defines as 'normal' areas like the economy, the spiralling crime rate, the passing of a new schools bill and a spirited public debate. Most South Africans I met are thankful for that.

While many, black and white, grumble about the new government and its failure to cope with crime and the economy, there is still a deep sense of relief that the past, with its institutionalized discrimination and its terrible political violence, has become a memory. To tell the truth, I had been afraid of going back. Too much happened in my life in South Africa for me to ever take the country for granted. I was afraid that I would feel out of place, a relic of a fast-vanishing era. Happily I was wrong, we still recognized each other. I know that my attachment was not simply the consequence of a particular story or period in history. It had to do also with friendship and memory, with land and people and the insistent voices of the heart. My favourite quotation from the Afrikaans writer Andre Brink, and I'll never tire of quoting it, says simply, 'The land that happened inside us, that nobody can take away from us, not even ourselves.' God Bless Africa. Nkosi Sikelele Africa.

CYNTHIA'S STORY

Tembisa, February 1999

White rule had been swept away, a black government was in power and Nelson Mandela was President. But, for many South Africans, little had changed; there was still extreme poverty and life was a constant struggle.

Her baby started crying the moment I approached. It wasn't a normal baby's cry, something much more frantic. Cynthia did her best to soothe the baby and then she apologized: 'I am sorry, Master, but she is afraid of the whites. When they came it was in the morning and we were still asleep.' My white skin had apparently reminded the infant of the white council workers who had come at dawn a few days earlier. The sleeping families had been driven out with shouts and threats and then the bulldozers crushed their tin shacks. Now Cynthia and her five children were living beneath a piece of plastic sheeting held up by a wooden stave. Every morning Cynthia buried the sheet in the ground. What could not be seen could not be knocked down.

That was South Africa in the winter of 1993, heading into the last year of white rule. Days of darkness, days of light. A country still fearful of civil war, yet high on hope for the future. Cynthia wanted a house. And a job and education and health care. Just somewhere for my children to sleep, Master, she said. Always calling you Master, the habit of a lifetime clinging on through the final moments of the white oligarchy.

I remember writing down the details of Cynthia's story. Another hard-luck story in a country full of hard luck. She had been abandoned by her husband two years before. He just walked out, she said, leaving her with the five children. Life had ground down to a simple routine of survival. Cynthia did not complain. She simply stated things as they were, as if poverty and abandonment had been implicit in her existence from the beginning. And yet she hoped somehow that Mandela and the ANC would lift her out of this. The good times would come, they surely would.

As I was leaving that night, fires were being lit in the camp. I looked back and saw Cynthia and her children huddled under the plastic sheeting. If freedom was to mean anything, I thought, it had to deliver for the Cynthia Mthebes of this world.

I thought of her again during the election. I wondered if she'd managed to join the long lines of people at one of the polling stations. With five children in tow it would have been difficult. Soon after that I left South Africa for good. But I thought often of Cynthia. Why her more than any of the other 'victims' I'd encountered down the years in South Africa? I guess it was that final image in the camp: the winter cold, the light from the fire, the children huddled close to her on the veld, the strange sadness of the hope she felt.

I had forgotten about Cynthia until the *Panorama* programme called me up and asked if I would return to South Africa. With the first elections under black rule due in a few months' time, the idea was to see how much life had changed for those at the bottom of the pile, the nearly fifty per cent of people who have no homes or jobs. I immediately thought of Cynthia Mthebe. It took about three weeks and a lot of searching but in the end a black colleague, Victor Mathom, eventually tracked Cynthia down. She was still living in the Tembisa area, he said, still living in the camps. And there were two more children to feed, Thomas and Thandi, grandchildren who'd been born since 1994.

And so on a southern summer morning six weeks ago I walked down a dusty track in Tembisa and shook hands with Cynthia Mthebe. She looked tired and her clothes were covered in dust. 'So what's changed?' I asked. Cynthia pointed towards a shack of tin and wood and told me it was her new home. Jammed in on either side were the other squatter shacks and beyond them a huge, odiferous rubbish dump. Squatterland is a place of bad smells. Sweat, excrement, paraffin, wet clothes, stale beer, fires of burning rubber. The smell of rubbish piled on street corners, of one room where seven people sleep. The smell of the very poor. Life had not really changed. The shack was better than the plastic sheet but no mother would want to raise children there. In the summer the rains flooded the bedroom. Everything got drenched. In the winter the wind rattled through the holes in the corrugated sheeting. There was no sanitation, only a hole in the ground which Cynthia dug herself. Nor was there any electrical current. Only twelve per cent of black South Africans have electricity. There was one big improvement. A water tap had been installed next to the shack. Cynthia shared this with her neighbours.

Her life revolved around the children – five of her own and the two grandchildren. To feed her family she worked on the nearby rubbish dump. Every morning at eight this fifty-six-year-old grand-mother climbed the hill to the dump to scavenge for tin cans. For every bag full of cans she received the equivalent of £3 – half of that had to be paid to the lorry which delivered them to the recycling depot. It could take up to three days to fill a bag. Dirty, exhausting work for a woman who suffers from diabetes and high blood pressure. I went with her several mornings in a row. There were perhaps thirty or forty people 'working' the dump, all of them leaning into the mounds of rubbish, pulling at it with sticks and hands. As they tugged and probed, the flies rose in small clouds. 'It's dirty, I get sick. But what shall we do? We want to put food on the table. We must work,' said Cynthia.

The life of Cynthia Mthebe revealed itself slowly. Over the following days I learned that her eldest son Jimmy had developed a serious drinking problem. He was in his twenties now with no steady job. I saw him a few times, sitting outside his shack next door to Cynthia. Jimmy smiled when you spoke to him, but his gaze always seemed fixed on some distant point over your shoulder. Another boy, sixteen-year-old Vincent, was mentally impaired. A beautiful-looking child who sat near the shack all day, his eyes flicking back and forth, never moving far from his mother's side. Vincent should have been in a special school. But Cynthia did not have the money to send him: it came down to something as basic as the bus fares. She just could not pay them. Her biggest worry was eighteen-year-old Amos. I had the feeling he was her favourite.

When I met him he was mending an old radio, head bowed in deep concentration. Like all of Cynthia's children he was soft spoken and polite. But Amos dropped out of school last year. He left without any qualifications. Nowadays he fixed radios and danced with a rap outfit. Cynthia feared for him. 'Sometimes he doesn't sleep at home, he just goes. He says he is going to his friends or to stay with his sister but I don't know. I worry because so many children are shot dead these days.' Her real worry is that Amos is heading for a life of crime. At least one of his old schoolmates is a well-known car hijacker. The gun is the route to wealth and power in the squatter camps and Amos, jobless and futureless, can see his old friends driving large, stolen cars, wearing expensive clothes and flashing large wads of cash. Cynthia wants him to go back to school and Amos says he will. But I doubted that he would.

Cynthia does have one other source of support. Her daughter Doris works as a domestic in the white suburbs of Midrand. Because she needs to live near work she must leave her young daughter with Cynthia. Doris only sees her child at the weekends. Millions of black women are in the same position. Doris dreams of living 'like the white people', in a big clean house. When I asked about her mother she started to cry. 'The worst thing is that my mother, she is always sick. I know if she is dead what am I going to do? She is trying to make my child live better and my sister's child live better. I am so ashamed because of them, those two little children.' Shame. Guilt. Humiliation. Failure. These were the bywords in Doris's life. A mother who could not live with her child, who could barely provide for her child. A mother who depended for survival on her own mother.

Cynthia has a plan though. She has put her name down for one of the government's new serviced sites. Here the homeless are given a toilet and a tap. There is a grant to buy bricks for a house. When I inquire about her progress the local council cannot find her name on the list. It has become lost in a bureaucratic tangle typical of the old and the new South Africas. But Cynthia will keep trying. There are three million plus squatters in the country but she will not give up. It will be a small house but with brick walls and a solid roof. A place without rain and flies and rubbish. A place where a good woman can rest at the end of the long day. Before I leave I tell Cynthia that a lot of people would think of her as a hero. Did she feel like a hero? No, she said, laughing. Oh, but you are, Cynthia Mthebe. You are.

CHRISTMAS IN CAPE TOWN

London, January 1999

**Christmas at the other end of the world. Spent under a warm sun,
close to the beach, in the shadow of Cape Town's Table Mountain.
A visit to church, lunch in a restaurant, some good conversation
and, for young Daniel Keane, a chance to see the baboons.**

We came home in darkness and cold. Lost to us the big skies, the
warmth and sunshine. Home to little streets, terraced houses and
the silence of Christmas roads. How forbidding and sad London
looks in the early dark, a city trudging cold and tired into the last
days of the year. At such moments I wonder why I am living here.
And I come up with just one answer: work. Just the work. What
a grim admission.

Sorry, Londoners, I try to like the city of my birth but it
really is a struggle, especially after Christmas in Cape Town. The
taxi-driver tried his best to console us on the way in from Heathrow.
He said the weather was mild compared to last week. Nine degrees
and holding. But what did he know? The day before as we flew
out of Cape Town it was hovering around thirty with the sun
glancing on the blue water at Camps Bay and the beach crowded
with the children of the southern summer.

Paragliders sailed over the rim of Table Mountain, their shadows
like the wings of giant hawks swooping down the mountain
towards the green suburbs. Out on the bay, ferries were plying
tourists back and forth to Robben Island on a calm sea. The political
prison where Nelson Mandela spent most of his twenty-seven
years in jail has become a tourist Mecca. When I first came to the
city in the early eighties Mandela was still in residence and tourists,
or any kind of visitors, would have been arrested for approaching
the island. How things change.

Having spent several weeks working in the dust and squalor of the squatter camps around Johannesburg, I was ready for Cape Town. I know that the city's critics deride it as an island of privilege in a country weighed down by the legacy of apartheid.

Driving in from the airport the traveller cannot fail to notice the vast squatter encampments which are separated from the city by the imposing bulk of Table Mountain. And, yes, some of the local whites are unbearably smug about their good life between the mountain and sea. Worse still are the new European arrivals who have bought vast houses and established themselves as a kind of imported gentry. 'Eurotrash' the locals contemptuously call them.

But none of my reservations can take anything away from the seductive beauty of the Cape. It is the landscape that draws me back time and again; landscape and, of course, the friendships forged in the darker days of the South African story. A Canadian friend who had gone to Kenya for Christmas gave us the use of his home on the slopes overlooking Camps Bay. Most days we took to the road, exploring the beaches and coves of the Cape coast: Noordhoek with its great expanse of white sand and blue water, Scarborough and Witsands where the light sea mist drapes the rocks and dunes in late afternoon, and Hout Bay where we spent Christmas Day.

It rained in the morning and Father Thornton's plans for an open-air mass were hastily abandoned. And so we crowded into the tiny church, to listen to the elderly priest's pious exaltations and breathe in the smoke of incense which his helpers liberally swept along the aisles. Being not remotely pious and an individual of some imperfection I always feel guilty when I go to mass. It is a sense that everybody around me is 'good' and that I am not. I am also an infrequent observer of Catholic ritual. My friend Father Dick, an Irish priest whom we met for Christmas lunch, said it didn't matter as long as you made the effort. But I am pursued by Catholic guilt and it took several glasses of good South African wine to rescue me from my sombre meditations.

I am happy to report that for the first time in my life I ate Christmas lunch at a restaurant. And also for the first time I did not eat turkey and ham. Such bravery at the age of thirty-seven! The small Italian restaurant on the beach was serving baked lamb and baby chicken. It was a long and happy lunch, one of the best Christmas Days I can remember.

There was only one depressing moment. An elderly German arrived at the restaurant accompanied by a large white dog. The man was old enough to have had an interesting past and his political opinions suggested a strong right-wing inclination. He told us the dog was a cross between a wolf and a husky. And then a black beggar approached. The dog growled menacingly. The German barely restrained the beast and shrugged the beggar away. 'If you want money, go and ask Mandela for it,' he barked.

It is the standard reply of the disgruntled white who cannot bear the reality of a black-ruled South Africa. Blacks knocking on white doors looking for jobs hear it all the time. It suggests, at the very least, a remarkable absence of humility on the part of the former ruling class. What do they think South Africa would have been like without Mandela and his gift of reconciliation and forgiveness? After several glasses of wine my capacity for indignation was ripe. I was about to read the Riot Act to our German friend when Father Dick pulled me back. 'It is Christmas Day, let it go,' he said.

He was right. Christmas Day is not a time for arguments. And so we climbed into Dick's car and headed for Cape Point in search of baboons. I had told my nearly-three-year-old that the Cape was full of monkeys and apes. The prospect of a meeting thrilled him greatly. But so far they had been noticeably reluctant about showing themselves. 'Where are the baboons, Dad?' came the insistent question every evening as we drove home after another apeless day.

Just outside Simonstown, on a narrow stretch of road between mountain and sea, we encountered a large family group. They sat in the road and stopped the traffic. The bolder ones climbed on to cars and began to beg for food. A bus full of Chinese tourists stopped directly ahead of us. Hands appeared out of the windows, one of them trying to stroke the head of a male baboon. We honked our horn furiously. A baboon's bite is particularly ferocious and they are, however familiar with humans, still wild animals. The Chinese were puzzled by our concern. It reminded me of an incident when I was living in South Africa in the early nineties and a group of Chinese visited a lion park outside Johannesburg. Two of the group got out of their vehicle and posed for a picture with the lions. The result: two dead Chinese tourists. But my son was delighted by the spectacle on the road ahead of us. Baboons on Christmas Day! Will he remember it when he grows up? I'd like to think he would but I suppose not. I will, though.

On the night before leaving for home we travelled out to the winelands for a barbecue on the farm of my friends Richard and Silvanna. Richard is a cameraman whom I came to know while living in South Africa. We still work together from time to time. But these days most of his efforts are taken up with fruit farming. It is as far away as you can imagine from battlefields and squatter camps. A saner life.

His farm sits below the Great Drakenstein mountain near the town of Franschoek. There are rows of peach and nectarine and apple trees. There are horses and some ducks and even some baboons and wild boar who raid the fruit orchards at night. As dusk came on, Richard lit the firewood and the great mountain above us melted into shadow. His four young boys disappeared into the fruit groves with our son. And we adults relaxed and opened some wine and spoke of old times on the road. It was Christmas all right but not like I'd ever known it.

A BOY CALLED 'GRENADE'

Kigali, Rwanda, April 1997

Today's correspondents meet many people who've suffered loss or been traumatized by war and violence. Sometimes it can prove an educational experience. This was the case when the author interviewed a young survivor of the Rwanda massacres which cost the lives of hundreds of thousands of people. He ended up questioning the very way he and other news-gatherers work.

Like nearly every other survivor of the genocide I have met, Placide always looked away when answering questions about what had happened to him. He did not look into my face, but rather into some unreachable distance, in whose limitless spaces he seemed lost. Yes, he could tell me his story and he could remember names, dates, places and incidents. But he would not meet my eyes and so that most fundamental of human contacts evaded me through the long hour I spent with him. Later, I would find out why. But only after I had made a very foolish and hurtful mistake.

We were sitting in the church where he had seen his parents murdered, where he had seen children's heads smashed and pregnant women disembowelled, where he had seen what no child should ever see. And as I have done before in other zones of conflict, in other ruined countries, I listened, asked questions and recorded. He was patient with me. Most survivors are incredibly patient. But it was at the end of a day of stories, a day when the stories seemed to get worse and worse and by the end, sitting there in the church, I think I had started to lose my concentration. This is not by way of an advance apology for the mistake I made, but rather an explanation of how one can lose the sense of what one is doing.

You see, earlier in the day, somebody had told me that Placide's nickname was Grenade; this because he'd had a grenade thrown at him during the massacre and the shrapnel had badly marked his legs. I was given to understand that he liked the name, that he had laughed when someone mentioned it. It was background information, the kind of thing you store away and maybe or maybe not use when writing the script. But I decided to ask Placide about the nickname; it just might prove useful in building a picture of his life after the genocide.

'I understand you have a nickname,' I said. For the first time in the interview he looked directly at me. 'Is it true that your nickname is Grenade?' I asked. Placide's eyes began to fill with tears, in a few seconds he was crying uncontrollably. A soldier who had been helping us to interpret stood and took him by the hand and led him outside. I knew within an instant that my question had deeply hurt the child. Perhaps in front of his friends he had to pretend to like the nickname, but it was clear now that he felt ashamed, marked out and different because of his wounds. Grenade. The name singled him out and I, for the sake of one thoughtless question, had summoned up all of the pain it caused him.

I got up from my seat and walked out of the church, into a garden where, three years before, I had walked among the recently murdered bodies of Placide's family and hundreds of other local Tutsis. The bodies had been buried and a gardener had planted some brilliant yellow flowers along the pathway. Late golden African light played across the valley beyond. I could hear only birdsong and the quiet sobbing of the little boy. I began to think of the times I had faced other victims of violence and misery and asked them questions which had made them cry. It happens all the time in the world of news and current affairs. Reporters like me arrive in a place like Rwanda or Belfast or Dunblane and we come into people's homes to hear and record their stories and many of them do weep and their testimony very often moves our audiences. But what happened with Placide has caused me to pause and question my questioning.

It has caused me to ask if the need to bear witness is worth the pain it can cause to others. For when we ask, 'How do you feel?' is it not a question calculated to probe and bring into the public domain the deepest emotions, and does the asking of such questions not impose upon us some responsibility for the emotional well-being of the person we are interviewing?

It is not the first time that I have asked this question, but never before has it been so acutely defined for me as in that Rwandan church. For I move on as other reporters elsewhere move on. But the people whose grief we disinter are left to their lives and memories. In my case, the reporting of genocide and man's inhumanity to man has brought me professional praise and awards and many letters of thanks from listeners and viewers. But you must forgive me if I say that in the Rwandan church I felt ashamed of myself and the hurt which my question had caused. Of course, the world in which I work is full of difficult questions, questions which often demand an answer. But let me say only that Placide has reminded me to think carefully before opening my mouth; he has reminded me that humanity must come before everything else.

HORROR IN THE MANGROVES

Sierra Leone, March 1999

**Ten years of civil war had left the people of Freetown brutalized
and desperate for the struggle to end. Rebels stood accused of
killing, maiming and raping thousands in their bid to topple the
government of President Ahmed Tejan Kabbah. His regime was
being defended by a West African force led by Nigerians.**

At first, I thought it was an animal. A beaten dog maybe. A
strangulated wailing sound which filled the hotel lobby. A sound
you could not escape, a sound full of bad news. I walked outside,
following the direction of the wailing. There, in the hotel garden,
near the glittering blue pool and the flame trees, a man in a red
T-shirt was begging for his life. He was surrounded by soldiers;
three of them, I counted, crowding in around him, pushing, then
punching and kicking. A dark trickle of blood flowed from a
wound in his neck. I walked towards them with one of my
colleagues but they kept punching the man. Then one of them
cocked his rifle and the man began to scream. I understood now
why he wailed so, it wasn't the beating, it was the expectation of
imminent death. The soldiers hustled him away, out of the hotel.

I did not run up and intervene. I did not throw myself into the
middle of that malevolent swarm. I would like to say I behaved
like a hero but I was too afraid. That is the kind of place Freetown
is these days: full of rage and brutality. You move slowly and
carefully. No sudden moves at checkpoints, stop when they tell
you to stop. And when they hustle somebody away at gunpoint?
Observe, note it all down, remember their faces, but take care not
to follow lest they offer you the bullet instead.

As it happened, the man survived, we saw him an hour later

151

by the beachfront. A hotel porter explained that the soldiers had found him fishing on the rocks at the back of our hotel. They accused him of being a rebel spy. He told them he was just fishing to feed his family. I don't know what saved him, but he was a very lucky man. For this ramshackle city on the golden peninsula is a place of murderous rumours and easy deaths.

We were down at the estuary, not far from the Aberdeen Bridge; it was early morning and the clam gatherers were out, wading in the shallows of the mangrove swamp. It was a beautiful morning full of haze and soft light, and the call of the birds brought to us on the wind from their resting-places among the mangroves. And then we saw a group of locals pointing at a spot almost directly beneath us. There was a human shape, bloated and twisted, neither black nor white, but a strange blue, green colour. We moved closer and saw that it was a man. His hands were tied behind his back and his legs were tied together. There were five bullet holes in his back. It was clear he had been severely tortured. The Nigerian soldiers who were escorting us were impressed. 'That will teach him to be a rebel,' one of them said. The one who said that was a nice man; he was quiet and cultivated and dreamed of quitting the army and studying sociology in college. And I had no doubt that had he been present during that poor bloated wretch's final hours he would have added his own bullet for good measure.

Freetown in the time of war. I have seldom been in a stranger place. It is where Graham Greene meets Joseph Conrad. At night, after the six o'clock curfew, the Nigerian officers would arrive for dinner, followed by their hungry and weary bodyguards. And then the girls: Jo Jo and Juliette and God knows how many others. In their teens and twenties, in the long dresses of much older women, they paraded in hope of business. But the hotel lacked the steady flow of customers which would have given them an income. And so the bored girls would come by our table and keep us posted on the latest gossip and rumours from the town. They were sad, sweet creatures. Jo Jo wanted out – badly. She produced her passport, which showed that she was twenty years old. In the photograph she was wearing a large West African wrap around her head. 'Hey, I look like a real African lady, huh,' she said, and then laughed at herself and at us and at the whole crazy situation. She said she had a German boyfriend but he had gone home. Jo Jo said he had promised to send for her and she believed him. She believed him.

Later at night we would sit and drink with the mercenaries. Neil, the white South African who flew the helicopter and Fred, Fijian Fred, the former SAS man and living legend who was his door gunner. I make no judgement on these men or their trade. They had crossed the line from mercenary self-interest into belief in the cause. Of course, they had seen the interior of the country, flying day after day over villages devastated by the rebels. After years in the country I guess they had seen enough of the massacres, amputations and sheer nihilism of the rebels to convince them that here, at the end of their mercenary days was a cause worth fighting for, something bigger than money. On our last night in Freetown, we bought some fish and cooked them in the moonlight just above the beach. Freetown was quiet as far as we could hear. But then the waves and the Atlantic breeze in the palm trees tend to drown out all but the loudest noises.

'What a country this could be,' said Fred. He was drunk now, but then so was everyone. 'What a country. With all its diamonds and fishing and all these lovely people. It could be such a country,' he said. I agreed with him and we all raised our glasses for a toast. And then I wondered what was happening on the other side of the bay at that moment. The part of the bay near the mangrove swamp where men are beaten and shot and heaved into the water. It wasn't that far away at all, just across the water in fact.

AN AFRICAN RENAISSANCE

London, March 1999

There had been hopes that Africa was witnessing the dawn of a new era of enlightenment; that the brutal despots of the past were being replaced by leaders of vision and compassion; that war and suffering were being consigned to history. But these proved to be forlorn hopes: the continent was still overwhelmed by corruption, poverty and violence.

And so another terrible few weeks for Africa. Weeks when the old 'heart of darkness' clichés galloped from one headline to another, when the tentative hope about an African renaissance vanished into the rainforest and even the most loyal friends of the continent struggled to put any kind of positive spin on the news from down below.

We have had thousands butchered in Sierra Leone, Hutu rebels murdering tourists in Uganda, Laurent Kabila arresting diplomats and locking up his political opponents in Congo, and God knows what kind of brutality and corruption across the river in Congo Brazzaville. Up in the Horn of Africa, Ethiopia and Eritrea are engaged in a full-scale war; Mugabe's goons are torturing journalists in Zimbabwe; and Daniel arap Moi's cronies are suggesting that the Kenyan constitution be abandoned and that he be allowed to run for a third five-year term.

I was going to stop with my examples there, but what the hell. Take a quick glance through the Africa news on any of the wire services and consider the sorry evidence.

I see that in Burundi the Tutsi army is rampaging once again; in Guinea the opposition leader is on hunger strike in prison; in Sudan oppression and suffering continue much as usual. Right in the heart of the continent something of the order of nine African armies are engaged in a major war for strategic dominance of the Great Lakes region. Nine armies and an ocean of miserable, terrorized civilians are being driven back and forth across the landscape by the rampant soldiery.

But if you confront any of the tyrants, they will invariably tell you that it is all the fault of colonialism. For sure, historical responsibility for the drawing of insane borders lies with the Europeans who caused the scramble for Africa; we know that the racism and greed of the colonial era created a dangerous mix of anger and inferiority; and that when independence came the people of Africa were, by and large, left to the mercies of a new ruling class that had neither the training nor the inclination to rule in a just or competent manner. And, yes, the Western powers and the Soviet bloc did their best to destroy Africa in the sixties and seventies by sponsoring their favoured dictators.

But at the end of all this, we are confronted with the responsibility of African leaders for African problems. To look back and blame outsiders may offer a measure of mental comfort, but it strikes me as being rather similar to the tactic of a child who has been brought up in an abusive home and blames the anti-social behaviour of his adult years on his parents. There comes a time when the past ceases to be an alibi, and here, at the turn of the twentieth century, we have surely reached that point.

The other familiar complaint is that the Western media only ever show the bad side of Africa, that we have a racist obsession with war and famine, that our reporting is based on outdated views of the continent. There is a partial truth in this view, but it tends to avoid the main issue.

I come from an island where the habit of murder has brought us massive media attention. For more than three decades, the news from Northern Ireland was invariably dominated by violence, the threat of violence and the attempts to end the violence. And while I have heard myself carping occasionally about the foreign media's obsession with the IRA and their loyalist enemies, I know they were right to focus on the violence and the suffering. That was the fundamental reality, and it affected the lives of hundreds of thousands of people.

Ireland's sectarian crisis was not the creation of the media, nor was it caused by journalists wanting to show only the bad side of Ireland. The same goes for the former Yugoslavia or any other troubled area.

The media can distort and misrepresent. They can make things worse. The absence of context and the oversimplification of issues (particularly in countries such as Rwanda) can create an atmosphere in which Western governments simply throw their hands up and refuse to engage with Africa. But please don't imagine that if we stopped reporting the famines and wars of Africa, they would disappear. They would be out of sight and out of mind but would, I suggest, be even more prolonged and vicious.

We face an utterly depressing reality in Africa. There are small moves forward here and there but a great ocean of suffering persists, which year by year eats away at hope, and pushes Africa and the Africans further away from our concern and interest.

Do you remember the 'African renaissance'? Just two years ago our pages were full of optimistic words about a continent that finally seemed to be pulling itself out of the mire. Do you remember the editorials and the features lauding the new African dawn? They seem embarrassing now.

How desperate we were to believe in the idea of a continent-wide rebirth, of an Africa whose leaders would prove just and decent and whose people would enjoy freedom from fear and hunger. The era of what Wole Soyinka called the 'Toad Kings' – Mobutu and friends – was over, we believed. The old monster was driven out of Zaire and died in exile but, surprise surprise, a new monster replaced him. We wanted to believe that Laurent Kabila was our kind of fellow, a new African who would bring stability and the rule of law to the Congo. And so we refused to acknowledge his dubious past; we embraced the politics of wishful thinking.

Kabila was just another despotic crook, but in our rush to believe in an African renaissance we supported him. Now that he has started locking up Western diplomats (he has been locking up his own people since he came to power), we start to ask questions about the nature of the regime we once enthusiastically supported.

The natural answer to all of this is to point to relative success stories in countries such as Uganda, or to mention Nigeria's recent transition to democracy. But, as Nigerian history has shown, it takes a great deal more than a successful vote to ensure the stability and viability of democratic institutions. Just ask the people of Kenya what difference having the vote has made to their lives, or whether it has hindered Moi and his cronies as they plunder the country.

The test is not at the ballot box but among the civil servants and soldiers and big businessmen, from whom real democracy should demand honesty. Corruption, and the greed it represents, are Nigeria's and Africa's greatest crisis.

The fundamental idea that underpins the Just Society – that government must rule for the common good – has been entirely subverted in much of Africa. The Big Men rule for the good of their families and their tribe. Only when the power elites find themselves being made accountable can we truly talk of African democracy.

There are no African quick fixes. But more than ever we need to engage with the continent, to support the governments that are trying to find a way out of the mess and to pressurize those who hold their people in contempt. Giving debt relief is one way of dealing with the problems of poverty, but only if we are sure that the people benefit and not the warlords. And more than anything we must engage at ground level among the organs of civil society where brave human rights activists and newspaper editors are fighting for justice. We must put our development money into grass-roots projects and steer it away from the crooks at the top.

Africa is full of brave men and women, people whose dignity leaves us feeling awestruck. It is time we recognized them as the real leaders of their countries.

SEAT OF THE PANTS

Angola, February 1998

Urgent stomach trouble necessitates a visit to the private lavatory of a government minister. And there's a new use for the reporter's notebook.

Somewhere between Johannesburg and Luanda my vaccination card disappeared. 'Surely that won't cause you any problems,' said my companion, Noah, as we stood in the immigration queue. 'You don't know these characters,' I replied, 'they'll use any excuse to shake you down.'

Sure enough a little man in a long white coat demanded to see our cards. 'It is lost, lost on the plane,' I explained, offering my best idiot's grin and urgently shaking his hand.

'Oh this will not do,' he said. 'We have laws. Something will have to be done.' He led me towards a room with a large fridge and on top of it – sweating in the equatorial heat – sat several containers of medicine. Beside them were numerous syringes and needles.

The man told me I had a serious problem. So serious that unless I paid him some dollars I would have to have an injection. He pointed towards his arm and then his posterior. The thought of subjecting my tender flesh to the mercies of this vulpine wretch induced tremors of fear.

He smiled. 'Sixty-five dollars would be the correct amount, Sen-hor.' I quickly paid up and he turned and went to the fridge. Inside, glistening in the cold, were bottles of whiskey and brandy and countless cartons of chocolates and cigarettes, the spoils of his one-man war against travellers.

'Welcome to Luanda,' I snapped at Noah as we drove through the crumbling suburbs. The city was as wretched a place as ever, except that now there were more restaurants and bars. Here the expat aid workers, the United Nations bureaucrats, the Portuguese businessmen and the Angolan elite mingle while the armies of street children wait outside hoping for stray dollars.

We had lunch at a Portuguese-owned café and I blithely told Noah he need not fear for his stomach. 'Somewhere like this you can be sure the hygiene is good.' Ah foolish, foolish me. That afternoon we went to the Ministry of Mines to interview the minister, Dr Marcus. Angola is rich in diamonds and other minerals but the resources were widely plundered during the war. The minister was midway through a tirade against diamond smugglers when my gut began to twist and tremble.

Sweat gushed down my face. Something terrible was happening in my stomach. 'Where is the toilet? Please, sir. Tell me where your toilet is,' I shouted at the minister. He jumped up with a shocked expression and opened a door to his left. 'In there, in there. This is my private toilet.' I hurled myself inside.

I looked around for toilet paper. There was none. I turned on the taps in the sink. There was no water. I tried to flush the lavatory. It was blocked. And this was the private toilet of the man who ran what should be the richest ministry in the country. 'Noah, I need your notebook,' I called out, my voice reduced to a snivelling whine. Seconds later several sheets of the BBC's best notepaper came gliding under the door. Having attended to the needs of decency, I thanked the minister and fled with what was left of my dignity.

We escaped Luanda and flew to Uige with the UN. The government and Unita fought prolonged battles here and I remember it as a frightening place during the war. Today an unlikely crew of Kenyans, Jordanians, Indians, Bulgarians and Russians are monitoring a ceasefire between the two sides. We were billeted at the main UN camp but the Russians had been mandated to feed us. We arrived at their house to find them in the middle of a mass hair-cutting session. They did not seem pleased to see us. 'Food, please,' I called out hopefully. Several 'Nyets' later and we were back on the street.

We survived thanks to the efforts of the wonderful Indian battalion, who, upon hearing we were from the BBC, prepared a stunning curry.

I must insert one word of praise for the Eastern Europeans. For without the intervention of a Bulgarian officer I might be cooling my heels in an Angolan jail.

At Uige airport Noah decided we should record some sounds for the documentary we were making. As we pointed the microphone towards a group of government troops one of them rushed over and accused us of being spies. It was a familiar tirade.

We were about to be marched off when Captain Boris appeared. He spoke in Russian. The soldier relaxed. Boris hugged him. Boris turned to Noah and explained. 'He was trained in the eastern bloc. I told him you were fine, that you were brothers of ours.'

The South African pilot of our light aircraft threw his eyes up to heaven upon hearing the story. 'It's like this all the time, man. But you know, you just get used to it.' Perhaps, my friend, perhaps.

FROM ELSEWHERE

FAREWELL TO HONG KONG

Hong Kong, July 1997

At the end of June 1997, China regained control of Hong Kong. After an emotional ceremony, the last British governor of Hong Kong, Chris Patten, sailed away on the royal yacht *Britannia*. It was the end of a century and a half of British rule.

The party is over. I'm not quite sure when it fully sunk in but it feels very strange. The restless city looks a little forlorn this morning. The fireworks have all exploded and gone. The *Britannia* is docked in the Philippines. China's soldiers, smooth-faced and silent, are standing guard at the Prince of Wales barracks, where, just a few days ago, the soldiers of the Black Watch posed for photographs with tourists. The monsoon doesn't help the mood. As I look upwards, yet more cloud, more rain is pushing in from the sea. I think the moment of absolute clarity, the unmistakable moment of change came for me when I drove past Government House this morning. The gates were closed. The first time I can remember that in the three years I've lived in Hong Kong. Inside the sentry box a couple of policemen were chatting and above them, sharply contrasting with the grey skies, the red flag of the People's Republic of China. A couple of tourists were standing at the gates peering inside. Just then I was reminded of Scott Fitzgerald's line from the end of *The Great Gatsby* when the dead romantic's house, where so many great parties were held, stands empty and his neighbour hears a car pull up to the gates. He wonders if this is some last guest who has come from the other end of the world but hasn't been told the party is over.

Well, those days are gone and forgive me if I sound a little wistful. I'm not an imperialist or a colonialist. Believe me, I've tramped around the wreckage of enough empires to recognize the fierce damage which they cause to subject peoples in Africa, Asia and the Americas. But the last five years of British rule, Mr Patten's time, were the most eloquent restitution for the evils of the past. And when he left, waving at the crowds on the quayside, I knew that something decent had been left behind. As he put it himself, 'the promise, the unshakeable destiny'. Now many say that he and Britain were wrong to try and democratize so late in the day when the British had for years denied Hong Kong any meaningful democracy. But what these short-sighted individuals cannot seem to grasp is that there is never a right time, never a respectable time for freedom because there can't ever be a wrong time when a man or a government or a people take liberty as their cause.

But this was not meant to be a political despatch. This really is a farewell note, for in a short while I'll be leaving Hong Kong to do another job. To be honest with you, I never thought I'd be sad to say goodbye. I remember my first day here, arriving from the brightness and warmth of a South African summer afternoon into the muggy grey of the south China winter. It was the week before Christmas and we spent the day, Christmas Day, in a borrowed flat with a small plastic Christmas tree on the table and a frozen turkey for dinner. We were homesick, longing for Africa and the friends we'd left behind and all the memories of the nearly five years we'd spent watching the country's transition to democracy. Back then I doubted that I'd ever be able to say I liked Hong Kong, much less feel any love for the place. And yet now, with the hour of departure bearing down on me like an injunction, I feel strangely out of sorts, bereft. I'm used to goodbyes but this one is very, very hard.

There are many reasons not to like Hong Kong: noise, over-crowding, materialism. But they are irritants, not the relentless curse some have called them. There was, there is so much else to the place that more than compensates for the aggravations of living in a small city into which six and a half million people have been crammed. For example, after South Africa, I found the almost total absence of crime a blessing. To be able to go to sleep at night, knowing that you don't have to worry about being mugged or murdered should not have to be a major plus in your life, but after South Africa it certainly was. Consider the fact that during the two major days of hand-over celebrations the Hong Kong police did not make a single arrest. That is, by anybody's standards, a remarkable statistic.

What will I miss? I will miss the eternally busy harbour, the Star ferry pulling away from the quay at Central and the lights of the Peak like a holy beacon twinkling far above. I will miss Hollywood Road and Cat Street with their ancient shops, crammed full of antiques and would-be antiques. And the old men sitting in the shade with their memories of China and the age of revolution and civil war and long marches and desperate escapes. I will miss the food, the great endless variety of it, those smells of garlic and ginger and chilli which filled the night-time streets and the sizzling of woks in kitchens hidden from the passing eye. I will miss Lantau Island with its sleepy fishing villages and green hills. And I will find it hard, most of all, to forget the kindness and the decency that I have encountered in so many people. They're not the rude, money-grabbing characters of popular cliché. Live here for any length of time and you will tap into the real nature of things. Yes, there is a hungering after the material but it is only a means to an end. A means of obtaining security. It is not the end in itself.

How could I forget you, Hong Kong? Here where my first child came into the world on a night in February when a thousand stars seemed to flicker across the water between Lantau and Lama and Hong Kong Island. When every ship bearing in from the South China Sea seemed, on that night, to be a harbinger of hope. How could I forget you? I never could, I never will.

LIVE AND LET DAI

Beijing, February 1996

Good company, a few beers, a highly recommended restaurant and dancing girls, too. Surely this was a recipe for a good night out?

At the very best of times I find Beijing a less than pleasant place. Interesting, yes. Culturally stimulating, yes. But pleasant or comfortable, never.

In the middle of winter, with a sand-gritted wind howling down from the Gobi desert. Beijing becomes a city of shrivelled, pinched faces, a place you will do almost anything to get out of. After you have visited the Forbidden City, Tiananmen Square, Mao's mausoleum, the Summer Palace and the Great Wall, the list of diversions peters out. If you are just a visitor with few Chinese friends, Beijing can soon close in around you like a cold, wet blanket.

Last winter I found myself trapped in the Chinese capital for a month and struggling, mostly in vain, to keep myself amused. One of the few consolations of those miserable weeks was exploring the city's numerous restaurants and the inexhaustible variety of Chinese food. I gorged my way from Szechuan to Hunanese to Shanghainese to Pekingese to Cantonese to Hainanese and back. Sitting behind plates of steaming food and gazing out at the snow whipping down the street, life in Beijing could seem tolerable.

Then came the night of the Dai restaurant.

I blame my friend Nin. It was he who promised a night of unforgettable cuisine and unprecedented entertainment.

Nin is a professional actor who divides his time between London and Beijing. A man given to grand gestures and rhetorical flourishes, Nin had that winter adopted a 'Heathcliff' look. His straight Chinese hair had been turned into something resembling wild curls which, with a scraggly beard and a raffish neckerchief, combined to make him look like a cross between the Last Emperor and Rab C. Nesbitt.

'What do you think? Very Bohemian, yes?' he inquired, as the taxi rattled towards the restaurant. 'It makes you look very dashing, Nin,' I offered. 'Ah dashing,' he sighed, and then, switching to Mandarin, he ordered the driver down a side lane. The restaurant was somewhere at the end of it. We passed a huge abandoned factory – Nin said the state had recently decided it would no longer underwrite its losses – and along a section of road where all the buildings had been levelled, Nin explained that these had been 'futons' – traditional dwellings of Chinese families, based around a central courtyard. They had been demolished to make way for yet another new hotel and shopping complex.

Several lanes later we finally arrived at the Dai restaurant. Gaudy streams of tinsel hung over the doorway and an old woman puffing on a cheroot emerged to welcome us. We followed her into the main dining room where a group of children sat in front of a blaring television set. They were transfixed by *Baywatch*, dubbed improbably into Mandarin.

The restaurant, like many others in Beijing, was owned by an officer in the People's Liberation Army – a true example of Deng Xiaoping's socialism. Beyond the main room was a series of 'special' guest rooms – small chambers where foreigners could pay extra for the privilege of shivering in a slightly smaller space.

We sat down and Nin delivered a series of orders, assuring me that I would never forget the cuisine. 'The best Dai food anywhere,' he said.

The old woman came back into the room. She coughed, went to the window and spat out into the darkened lane. I hoped nobody was passing at the time. She clapped her hands and called for silence. 'Now it is time for the special Dai dance. All included in the price,' she announced.

The door opened and three teenage girls shuffled in. All wore sullen expressions and were conspicuously overweight. The crone addressed them sharply and they stood to attention. They wore what appeared to be traditional costumes – lengths of blue and red material held together by safety pins. The old woman pressed the play button on a ghetto blaster which one of the girls had carried in. A strange music issued forth, high-pitched and, to my ears, somewhat tuneless. The three girls began shuffling back and forth, wiggling their hips with expressions of profound boredom. It was an agonizing display, and when it had finally limped to a conclusion I gave Nin a dirty look. He simply beamed back.

The agony was only beginning. Several beers arrived and one of the young men who had been glued to *Baywatch* came in. He was carrying a live turtle, whose tiny flippers flapped wildly as it was held aloft in front of us. The waiter grinned wildly and we smiled back. I foolishly thought this was his pet and he had brought it in to be admired.

With a triumphant shout he dropped the creature on the floor, jumped in the air and came crashing down on the turtle's back. There was a vile squelching sound as the amphibian entered the great ocean in the sky. The entire table groaned. Even Nin seemed horrified. 'I think it is one of their traditions,' he said weakly.

Some of our group wanted to leave but I felt sorry for Nin. I ordered more beer and more beer, and soon we had put the unpleasant business of the turtle behind us. We sang Irish ballads and Nin chipped in with a few dirties from his days as a 'volunteer' farm worker during the Cultural Revolution. There was yet more beer as we munched through a mountain of noodles and vegetables.

The waiter reappeared and announced that the special dish of the night was about to be served. A large bowl was put in front of me. There, sitting in its own juices, was the turtle – boiled and seasoned.

The waiter gestured towards the soup spoon. 'Very good. Very good. You will like it' he declared.

. I lifted the spoon, closed my eyes and sipped tentatively. The broth was lightly flavoured, like a blend of chicken and pork with hints of ginger and garlic. Perhaps it was the influence of the beer but to me it tasted delicious. I looked up at the waiter and told him that I had never eaten so tasty a soup. The others looked at me as if I had committed murder. 'How could you do that?' an Australian colleague hissed.

'Oh quite easy. You just put it in your mouth and swallow,' I replied.

The waiter went around the table and worked his intimidating magic, standing over each of the party until they had agreed to take some soup. Within minutes the uncomfortable silence had been replaced by the sound of a great collective slurp as the turtle slipped down our throats towards eternity.

The waiter left the room and a few moments later we could hear uproarious laughter from the room next door.

Another Beijing night was coming to an end.

WISH YOU WERE HERE

Afghanistan, August 1997

For a foreign correspondent, providing coverage of a war is probably the most physically and mentally challenging of all assignments. Working in Afghanistan, as the rebel army of Ahmed Shah Masood prepared to march on the capital, proved a surprisingly amiable if uncomfortable experience.

I woke up this morning dusty, stiff, hungry and thirsty and realized that Jonno's bug had made a long-feared migration. I have acquired little red bites that begin just above the elbow and continue all the way down to the fingertips. So far I have counted thirty-five of them. The itchiness is indescribable. They respond to no known medication. Jonno, a cameraman with Associated Press television, was the first to be attacked, bitten in the dead of night. He has now suggested that we douse our arms in petrol in an effort to kill them off before they begin to discover tastier parts of our bodies.

I am writing this on the floor of a mud hut which I am sharing with four other people and countless insects. Apart from Jonno, there is a photographer from France whom we call, strangely enough, Frenchie; and my two colleagues, Fred Scott from California and Joan Chang from Singapore. We are a multi-cultural little group, crammed in together into this small hut in the village of Golbahar close to the latest of Afghanistan's frontlines. Now, I have stayed in some fairly basic accommodation in my time but Club Golbahar, as we've named it, defies grading. In the other two rooms are several soldiers from the army of Ahmed Shah Masood and a Taleban prisoner whom, out of pity, they've adopted, giving him the job of keeping the place as clean as nature and the presence of a large group of men would allow.

172

The prisoner is delighted with this arrangement, it keeps him out of jail and if he behaves he will be given a job in the army for he is young, perhaps no more than twenty, and rather confused. Wrenched away from the brotherhood of extremism, he is struggling to come to terms with a world in which women are allowed to walk in the street, go to school and work in the fields. I think he is also lonely and misses his family. Once, my colleagues found him crying behind the building, not a typical gesture in heavily macho Afghanistan. When they passed, he covered his head with the blanket which is his sole possession.

One evening, as Jonno was playing one of his interminable disco records on the portable CD player we had brought with us, the officer in charge of the building called the prisoner over. 'Now you dance,' he said to us. Jonno obliged with a few steps and the major laughed. 'You see,' he said to the Taleban prisoner, 'there's nothing wrong with dancing and enjoying yourself.' Soon the prisoner began to imitate Jonno's prance and when he smiled, the major clapped and laughed.

That's the light-hearted side of Club Golbahar. Now for the grimmer details. For a start there's the dust that covers everything and everyone. Living in a mud hut in the blazing temperatures of high summer, this is not surprising but it is, to put it mildly, aggravating. We are covered in it from morning until evening, when we wade into the river to wash. Then we enjoy a few minutes of blessed cleanliness before the insidious dust clouds over us again. Then there are the insects, the biting bed bugs which first attacked Jonno and have since developed a taste for the rest of us. There are the armies of flies which cover our food and our faces. At night, we cover our heads with our shirts so that we won't wake up to find that our faces have become the Heathrow Airport of the local fly community. And of course I couldn't forget to mention the scorpions. This being high and dry territory, there are huge numbers of them scuttling around. The Afghan soldiers find them greatly amusing. One of their favourite games is to hold them up in front of our faces or hurl them at us in the dark just to watch us shriek and jump. All good, clean Afghan fun. Our greatest terror is that we will encounter one of these vicious insects as we're crouched over the hole in the ground that is our lavatory. To get to it, we must descend the steep stairs which are set into the mountainside. It is a dark, dank stomach-churning place about which the less is said the better. Unfortunately the regularity of diarrhoea amongst our happy little band necessitates regular excursions at all hours of the day and night. The 'runs' are an inevitable part of travelling in this part of the world, more especially if there's a war going on.

To try to avoid becoming really sick we must boil and filter all our water. It's a tedious chore and, with the heat, we're consuming vast quantities of water. For food, we are dependent on what can be rustled up from the market. There is, thankfully, a regular supply of tomatoes, onions, aubergines and potatoes and these, supplemented by various tins we have brought with us, keep hunger at bay. It's not gourmet cooking, especially with me as chef, but after a day at the frontline one is generally so exhausted that anything which tastes remotely edible is quickly wolfed down.

We have accumulated quite a retinue: there is Jamsha, the translator who dreams of escaping to America; there is Farine, the secret policeman who chops our vegetables each night while keeping a close eye on our movements; there is Darood, who came back from America to see if he could help his country recover from the war and now guides journalists around the frontline. Darood is a rare human being, a decent compassionate man in a time and place where these qualities are tragically lacking. And there is the major who wants to get to the capital, Kabul, so that he can see his wife and child. For a while, we were sad together. 'Do you think we'll get to Kabul soon?' he asked me. I told him I was sure we would, but I don't know if he really believed me. In this war people have their dreams but each day they recede; they slip away incrementally until all that is left is the illusion and, robbed of substance, it too eventually disappears.

But that is sad talk and our days in Club Golbahar have not been sad. We've laughed a great deal and I've made some new friends. So tonight, after flying into Pakistan, where I'll enjoy a bath, dinner and a good night's sleep between clean sheets, I'll send this message to Jonno, Frenchie, the major and Darood: 'Goodnight, boys, wishing you were here!'

A TALE OF TWO DENTISTS

Jerusalem, April 1998

The last thing a correspondent needs while away on assignment is toothache. The blinding pain it can bring is not conducive to good reporting. So when it struck the author while he was working in the divided city of Jerusalem there was only one, tiny consolation: it meant he could compare and contrast the treatment he received from two different dentists, one an Arab, the other a Jew.

I woke somewhere between the first call of the muezzin and the slow rattle of the delivery trucks rolling down Saladin Avenue. Jerusalem, still dark, was stirring and my head was threatening to explode with pain. The offending tooth had been nagging for several weeks and I had told myself that once back in London I would enter the steely embrace of the dentist's chambers. Foolish me. I had barely set foot in the Holy Land when the pain escalated from amber to red alert. Through the dusty wastes of the Gaza Strip, through the old city of Jerusalem and on through Tel Aviv and back up to the West Bank, the agony increased. Israel and the Occupied Territories, at the best of times, demand a calm eye and a cool head. I am afraid that for much of the trip I saw everybody – Palestinian officials, Jewish settlers, Israeli soldiers, Hamas leaders – through the twisted prism of a grade-A toothache. To describe my private emotions as, let's say unsympathetic, would be an understatement.

Back in my Jerusalem hotel room in the restless hours before dawn I was pacing the floor and cursing my stupidity. I have lived in fear of dentists all my life, a relic of a ghastly incident when I was seven years old and an elderly tooth-puller yanked out one of my teeth without the benefit of anaesthetic. By seven a.m. the morning shift had arrived at reception and they swiftly recom-

176

mended a dentist; this being Arab east Jerusalem they pointed me towards a small building around the corner from the hotel, to a Palestinian dentist. Dr Abu Libdeh worked on his own. 'You like Irish music?' he asked after guessing my nationality. When I answered in the affirmative, he pressed a button and the theme music from Titanic filled the room and I, contemplating his drills, began to get that sinking feeling.

I closed my eyes and tried to think of Ireland but I learned, as do most visitors here, that conversations in Jerusalem tend to work their way towards land and politics. And so it was that Dr Abu Libdeh told me the story of his family, now living in the United States. They had lost their lands in the 1967 war when the Arab armies attacked Israel. The Arabs suffered a humiliating defeat and lost east Jerusalem and the West Bank. The doctor was not a fanatic, he was a sad-eyed man. Something suggested that he knew that whatever the outcome of peace talks there could be no going back to the world that he knew as a child. His family would never return, there would be little welcome for them in the Jewish state. He asked me about Ireland. Were the 'troubles' there anything like those of the Jews and Arabs? I mumbled through the anaesthetic something about all situations being different. The usual non-committal 'keep to the safe ground' formula for countries which, to use Seamus Heaney's immortal line, are full of 'open minds, as open as a trap'. Whatever you say, say nothing.

I paid the melancholy dentist and said goodbye. My pain was gone and the sun was shining. Foolish me. Eight hours later I was back facing the drills and the mouthwash of a new dentist. The pain had come screaming back that evening. Dr Abu Libdeh's offices were dark and shuttered and so, gibbering with pain, I made my way to the suite of a dentist in Jewish west Jerusalem. Dr Jacob was an orthodox Jew, a fanatical follower of Chelsea Football Club and he came from my home town of Cork. The family had left when he was young, moving to London before he decided it was time to come to Israel. In the background the music of Cat Stevens was playing: 'Tea for the Tillerman'. I wondered if Dr Jacob knew that Mr Stevens had since become a devout Muslim and is now known as Yusuf Islam. 'Really,' he said as he approached with his needle.

Dr Jacob was patently a kind and decent man. He stayed behind after hours to take care of my teeth. But he didn't have much time for journalists in general or the BBC in particular. 'You are biased against Israel,' he said as he carefully excavated the decay in my tooth. I tried to tell him that the media is often accused of bias, and that people often watched our reports through the filter of their own prejudice. But, to Dr Jacob, Israel was under siege and the media were on the side of the Arabs. He had voted for Binyamin Netanyahu because he didn't trust Shimon Peres. Now Netanyahu seemed to be bogged down. 'I thought he would push the peace process on our terms. But now there doesn't seem to be any peace process,' he told me. But if disillusioned with Netanyahu, Dr Jacob has a paranoiac mistrust of Yasser Arafat and the Palestinians. He now finds it increasingly difficult to discuss politics with his more liberal friends. I tried to imagine him sitting down and talking with Dr Abu Libdeh – what they would have to say to each other once the professional pleasantries were out of the way.

Like Dr Abu Libdeh, Dr Jacob asked me what I thought of the situation. I decided to be honest with him. I told him it appeared pretty hopeless to me, that the atmosphere between Arab and Jew in Jerusalem seemed to crackle with hatred. Not all Arabs, not all Jews but enough of a critical mass to make peaceful co-existence a rather distant prospect. Dr Jacob might easily have taken offence at that, but instead he smiled and said, 'Maybe so, maybe so.' And what can I say in conclusion except that thanks to the efforts of two dentists, one an Arab, the other a Jew, my last night in Jerusalem was a calm and painless one.

AGONY ON THE PILGRIM TRAIL

Santander, April 1999

Last time, toothache swooped during work time, while on a reporting assignment in the Middle East. On this occasion, it made its presence felt on holiday, during a journey with friends to the Spanish holy city of Santiago de Compostela. Finding a dentist had been much easier in Jerusalem . . .

The agony peaked somewhere off the coast of France. The slow agonizing throb that had begun in the base of my tooth now pounded throughout my head. It was the same tooth that had sent me scurrying to an emergency dentist in Jerusalem last year, the same tooth that had reduced me to a whimpering, snivelling wreck in North Carolina in January and now threatened to destroy a long-planned holiday in Spain. My travelling companions were a policeman, a Catholic priest and a marine biologist – all useful men in their own way but not in the matter of dentistry. Father Dick offered a few prayers for pain relief but soon tired of my misery and sprang out of his bunk when the others suggested a retreat to the bar. 'Offer it up to the Holy Souls,' were his parting words. Nor was the French ship's doctor up to much. He seemed upset that he had been called from his rest to deal with me: 'Take zeese,' he said, handing me a few codeine with an imperious flourish and then indicating the door.

By the time we reached Santander I had entered a world beyond pain, a high plateau of screaming nerve ends. My face had now swollen to a grotesque size and my friends agreed that something had to be done. This was a big city and there would surely be many dentists. A friendly pharmacist pointed us in the direction of a warren of back streets where, she assured me, there would

179

be many tooth-pullers and drillers only too happy to help. Confident that the calvary of the cavities was about to end I led the way as we climbed the steps to the first surgery we came across. Father Dick assumed his most pious expression and knocked on the door. There was no answer. I knocked, a more forceful thump than that of the holy man. There was a shuffling noise, the sound of a key being turned in a lock. A rather surprised-looking dental nurse appeared, fixing her hair. I remember only the word 'Mañana' – tomorrow, come back tomorrow, she told us. Argument was futile and so we retreated.

At this point let me enter a note of Euroscepticism. Before setting out on this journey we had all been whining about England and its rules and regulations and what we imagined was the terrible seriousness of people's lives. How nice it will be to wander among those laid-back continentals, we thought, to shake off the rigours of our clock-obsessed lives. Three dentists later, three 'I am sorry we don't open until this afternoon' excuses and I was longing for those solid grey shores. I was imagining with fondness the face of my White City dentist looming above me with a whirring drill. 'At least they go to work in the morning in England,' I snapped at the uncomprehending Spaniard who had just turned us away.

On the fourth try we knocked on a door in a shabby apartment building only to hear a furious husband/wife argument raging beyond. Eventually the door opened and an elderly couple stood facing us: she in her dressing gown, he fumbling with his cufflinks. They smiled serenely, the argument forgotten. 'Mañana,' he said and shook his head.

At the dentist after that – number five – the attendant looked at us as if we were fools. 'Not a chance today, maybe later in the week,' she barked. I had performed an elaborate pantomime of pain for her, but it made no difference. Suddenly the Spanish enthusiasm for the torments of the Inquisition began to make sense, even to the pious Father Dick, who up till now had maintained a face of perfect patience. There was no answer from dentist number six. I suggested that we go to a pharmacy and purchase some pain-killers. 'There might be more chance of getting a dentist in one of the country towns,' I said. But Father Dick insisted we press on. I hoped he was using his heavenly connection, that he knew something the rest of us could not see. But Dick was right: at dentist number seven we struck lucky. A smiling attendant answered the door and ushered us in. She spoke no English but Dick managed to mumble enough Spanish to explain my predicament.

A few minutes later I was shown into the surgery. There was an x-ray and injections and some scraping and pulling. After he had done his work I told the dentist I was on my way to Santiago de Compostela with my friend the priest outside. 'We are on a pilgrimage,' I said. It was at this point that I suspect he mistook me for a priest. For he was suddenly very impressed and extremely solicitous. He gave me some pain-killers – they looked like pills a horse might swallow – and antibiotics and assured me the agonies were at an end. As we were leaving I asked how much I owed. 'But you are pilgrims, I will not charge you,' he said. As an afterthought the good dentist suggested we might, somewhere along the route, say a prayer for him. He can rest assured – I haven't stopped praying for him.

A RAW HORSE IN THE MOUNTAINS

Kyushu, April 1998

Perhaps he shouldn't have turned down the horse sashimi! On a visit to Japan, a herbalist is needed urgently and a colleague must face retribution.

It cannot have been the horse sashimi. When the delicate slivers of raw horsemeat were introduced – 'local delicacy' the Japanese chef explained – I politely declined. The man seemed upset and I told him that I was a vegetarian.

It was a deliberate lie. I could not tell him that when I looked at the plate of bright red flesh I could see golden manes blowing in the wind, proud palaminos galloping on the high mesas, mares and their foals munching grass in the twilight. For me, raw horse is a meat too far.

As my colleagues tucked in I concentrated instead on the bean curd. It was bland but well-cooked and unlikely ever to be seen cantering around a paddock. But by mid-afternoon I could sense something had gone terribly wrong.

'Find me a toilet now,' I shrieked as the van wound its way through the main trunk road that skirts the mountains and volcanos of Kyushu. My stomach was churning with agony, sweat streamed down my forehead.

Readers will be familiar with my previous incident of stomach disaster in Angola. On that occasion I found myself gripped by gastric terror in the office of a government minister. His personal lavatory refused to flush and he had no toilet paper. On reflection, I seem to spend an inordinate amount of time finding clean lavatories as the after-effects of foreign cooking wreak havoc on my gut. Ah, the lost hours in Kigali, Kinshasa, Kalimantan . . . I could go on.

After driving for another fifteen agonizing minutes we eventually pulled into a restaurant where I exploded out of the van and disappeared into the toilets. My colleagues made polite conversation with the owner until, partially relieved, I returned to be introduced to the owner's wife, Mrs Iwota.

'This is the woman who'll sort you out,' said my colleague David 'Tubby' South. In retrospect, I should have been suspicious. There was something altogether too concerned about Tubby's expression.

Mrs Iwata, he explained, was a herbalist and a healing masseuse. Under normal circumstances I am deeply suspicious of alternative medicine. But these were anything but normal circumstances. I was offered a cup of steaming green liquid and told to drink.

'That is green herb drink. Special herb. Very good tumtum,' said the wife. She patted my gently sloping stomach. I drank the beakerful of warm liquid and almost collapsed. As she watched me struggle not to retch, Mrs Iwota smiled: 'I see it having good effect.'

I don't know that I have ever drunk anything more foul or poisonous – and I have drunk a great many strange liquids. I imagined it as a mixture of pig slurry and the sweat from a sumo wrestler's jock strap. However, worse was yet to come.

Mrs Iwata ordered me into a side-room and told me to lie down. The room was packed with local farmers preparing to take part in a dance festival. They stopped what they were doing and gathered around to watch the healing performance. There was a worrying amount of snickering and nudging.

Mrs Iwata began to unbutton my trousers. I was about to make my excuses and leave when her hand delved into my groin, causing a sharp stab of pain. I howled and the farmers laughed delightedly.

Behind them I saw the smirking faces of Tubby and the rest of·

the crew. They produced a camera and began to film my agony.

For twenty minutes Mrs Iwata pressed and twisted my stomach. When I had been reduced to a gibbering ninny and the farmers were exhausted from mirth she told me to stand up.

I duly rose and, apart from feeling a little light-headed, I could feel none of my earlier symptoms. Whatever was in her green liquid, whatever the strange manipulations of my gut, the sweats and the spasms had vanished. Mrs Iwata had proved as good as her word.

But there was still the matter of Tubby to be sorted out. He had clearly taken far more pleasure than was natural in my discomfort. Retribution was certainly called for.

That night we joined the Iwatas and their farmer neighbours for a barbecue: fine ordinary steak with not an equine sliver in sight. I slipped away from the table and found Mrs Iwota in the kitchen. 'My friend Tubby San has a very bad back,' I explained. 'He really wants a strong massage but he is too shy to ask you.'

Mrs Iwata smiled; that same unsettling smile I had seen earlier in the day.

'Leave him to me. I fix him,' she purred.

A few minutes later Tubby was summoned from the table. 'Now is your turn,' said Mrs Iwata, her voice shimmering with menace. When the cameraman attempted to bluster, our producer Bill – a man of courtly charm and ruthless determination – declared that it would be dreadful manners to refuse the offer.

My last memory is of Tubby groaning on the floor as the small, fierce hands of Mrs Iwata prepared to descend.

THE IMPOSSIBLE CHOICE

London, March 1999

Life was already difficult for Burma's pro-democracy campaigner Aung San Suu Kyi. With the rest of her family in England, she was under house arrest and facing constant harassment by the military authorities. Then came news that her husband was dying. The Burmese refused him permission to come to her. Instead they suggested that she should fly to London. It meant she had to make a choice between her campaign for freedom or her dying husband.

So think about this for an impossible choice. You are the leader of a movement for freedom that is harassed and attacked at every turn by a despotic military regime. Millions of people look up to you as the symbol of their struggle. You have endured years of house arrest, and seen your best friends imprisoned and tortured, your people murdered and driven from their homes. And as I say, you are the one figure who remains capable of giving your people hope.

The military regime knows that if there were a democratic election in the morning, you would be President of the country. The reason they know it is that elections have already been held in which you won an overwhelming victory. The problem is that they refused to accept the result. Their attempts to destroy your spirit take many forms. There has been the aforementioned house arrest and persecution of your allies. But there is also something more insidious: a campaign against your family that is designed to make your personal life a torment. They refuse to allow your husband or your two sons to enter the country and visit you. In fact they have gone so far as to strip your sons of the citizenship that is their birthright.

And then you learn that your husband, the man who has raised the boys while you have been under house arrest, is dying from cancer. He is in England and you are in Burma. You know that the Burmese authorities want to deport you, would do anything to get you out of the country. And so they refuse your dying husband permission to come and visit you, insisting that you leave and visit him instead. They say they are concerned for his health and fear he would not survive the journey. Words such as 'irresponsible' are used. Quite correctly you surmise that the generals want you gone and are willing to use the tragedy of your husband's poor health to achieve their aim. And if you do leave, you leave behind the millions who are suffering, those for whom you are the only hope.

But your husband, as quiet and gentle and decent a man as was ever born, is dying. He longs to see you and you long to see him, and that is the loneliest, most impossible dilemma to confront anybody.

I know Aung San Suu Kyi well enough to know what pain she must be feeling. Of all the world leaders I have met I can think of no other who is more visibly humane or more deeply touched by compassion for the suffering of others. Her own privations she endures with stoicism and the strength of her Buddhist faith. But it is the fate of those who suffer because they have followed her dream of freedom, or who have aligned themselves with her, that most concerns Aung San Suu Kyi.

And Michael Aris, her husband and the father of her sons Kim and Alexander, has been badly persecuted. As he would doubtless affirm himself, the choice was one he made willingly and with eyes wide open. From the very outset Suu made it clear that the freedom of her country and people was the foremost goal of her life.

Those who know Michael will be aware of just how deeply he himself is committed to the Burmese struggle. I know it myself from numerous conversations; when I last saw him, at a dinner party more than a year ago, he was full of plans and ideas. But he is a shy and private man who has always refused to parade himself in public, concentrating instead on quiet campaigning and the essential work of raising the couple's sons.

That has been the true measure of his love for Suu and his commitment to the Burmese struggle.

They met and married while she was a student at Oxford, moving first to the Kingdom of Bhutan and then travelling back to Oxford where Suu gave birth to Alexander and Kim. And then in the late eighties came the moment when the family's life was changed for ever. Suu's mother became seriously ill and Suu returned to Burma to act as her nurse.

Her return coincided with the rise of a mass democracy move-ment, and she emerged from her mother's home in Rangoon to lead it. As a lifelong evangelist for democracy, and the daughter of the country's founding father, Aung San Suu Kyi was the natural choice to lead the movement. There followed a brutal crack-down in which thousands were killed, then an election which her League for Democracy won – and then the military rejection of the result. The rest is a history of repression that has lasted until this day.

I have not seen Aung San Suu Kyi in more than three years. (The last time I applied for a visa the Burmese authorities made it clear that I was not welcome.) When we did meet she spoke about Michael and the boys, and the pain of separation. But it is not a topic she likes to dwell on; she simply described the separation as 'difficult' and reminded me that thousands of Burmese families were going through similar pain.

We spoke a lot about Nelson Mandela and she agreed with his comment that one of the most difficult things for the leader of a pro-democracy struggle was the pain suffered by their loved ones.

'I felt exactly the same way about my sons,' she told me. 'To tell the truth I tried not to think about them too much because that didn't help. I just thought, they've got a good father and they will be all right.' Now that the good father is stricken with illness I cannot speculate on what Suu or her children will be feeling. But you and I can imagine what we would feel ourselves in the same situation. We can only pray to high heaven that we never find ourselves in that sad place.

But we are also free to ask ourselves what kind of regime would refuse a dying man permission to visit his wife. Think of the meanness of spirit that that implies. In fact, I understate this: think of the cruelty and malice it takes. Now, if we were talking about someone who had sworn to bring down the military by a violent revolution in which the generals would perish, you could perhaps see a point to their behaviour. But we are talking about a woman who preaches peace and really means it. No half-truths, no evasions, no hidden agendas. Agree to democracy, she says, and there will be no recriminations and no witch-hunts. That is the promise, and I believe her. The generals have no idea how lucky they are to have a leader-in-waiting of the calibre of Aung San Suu Kyi.

But they do not see it that way. They see democracy as signing the death warrant to their regime of exclusive power and they cannot believe in a human being who is not governed by greed and megalomania.

If they continue to refuse a visa, then the world is entitled to make its own judgement. The world, and particularly Burma's Asian neighbours, will be entitled to say that there is no way back for these people, that they must be shunned and excluded and sanctioned.

It need not be so. As the former British ambassador to Burma, Martin Moreland, put it this week: 'By making a gesture of compassion they could in fact help to bridge the gap between themselves and the pro-democracy movement.'

And so the choice is not one for Aung San Suu Kyi herself to make. She must not be asked to choose between her right to remain in Burma at the head of her people's struggle and her right as a wife to be with her husband in his hour of need. It is the generals who must now make the only decent choice there is: to give Michael Aris a visa and do it now.

Postscript

The regime never did grant Michael Aris a visa. Shortly after the publication of this piece he died from cancer. He was as kind a man as I've ever met. The moral pygmies who refused to give him a visa would never understand that kind of goodness. At the time of writing Aung San Suu Kyi is still continuing the struggle for freedom in Burma. It is not easy and these look like particularly discouraging times. But freedom will come. Of that you should have no doubt.

SPOILED IDEALISM

London, September 1998

The President of the United States was in deep trouble. Impeachment loomed over his affair with the White House intern Monica Lewinsky. And yet the American public continued to support him . . .

Throughout the past few days in America, I kept coming back to a phrase once employed by a biographer of the novelist F. Scott Fitzgerald. The biographer was linking the alcoholic Fitzgerald to his most famous character, Jay Gatsby, the boy from the wrong side of the tracks who had made good and then been destroyed by his own reckless passion. 'Spoiled idealism' was how the biographer described the descent of novelist and character from the promise they once held out, into the sorry defeat and destruction of their later lives. Spoiled idealism. Promise turned to betrayal, hope turned into something bitter. That was what we witnessed in America this week as a lying President hobbled from one embarrassing public moment to another. There is one encounter in particular which stands out. Clinton standing beside the Czech President and human rights hero Vaclav Havel at a Washington news conference. A woman reporter goes directly to the point: 'Do you still believe, Mr President, that you have the moral authority to lead this country?' Clinton's answer was, as ever these days, unconvincing. What was more interesting was the body language, the expression on his face. 'Of course I don't,' it said, 'but I'm damned if I'll admit it and damned if I'll do anything about it.'

What we are learning is that like the shabby dictators of the Third World whom he professes to despise, Mr Clinton cares more about himself than he does about the notions of democracy and accountability. Set beside a figure like Mr Havel, the American

President was reduced to what he truly is: a mendacious chancer who deserves to be driven from office. There are those who have argued that Mr Clinton deserves compassion, that we must not rush to judge a man because he had an extra-marital affair and then lied about it. I couldn't agree more. But the media Friends of Bill in this country miss the point. The scandal and the stink are about a great deal more than Monica Lewinsky. At the root of it all is contempt for the ideal of justice which we are told makes America great, and a betrayal of the ideals which Mr Clinton insisted he stood for when he was first elected back in 1992.

This, we are repeatedly told, is not like Watergate. It is not about the abuse of power. Clinton is not Nixon. I think he may in fact be something worse. With Nixon there was never any doubt that we were dealing with a political 'operator' as distinct from a visionary leader in the mould of JFK or Franklin Roosevelt. He never said it himself but America knew it was dealing with a political short-timer who refused to embrace big ideas but kept to a narrow, and ultimately terribly crooked, idea of what leadership and governance meant. Nixon was driven from office because he abused his powers. He used the state's security services to hound those he hated, he presided over crooked electoral finances and dirty tricks and allowed his subordinates to act as if they and the entire executive branch were above the law. When Watergate happened it simply confirmed what the political elite had known all along: the man was a crook who didn't deserve to sit in the White House. Nixon got the treatment he deserved.

Clinton began as the man from Hope who would return America to the politics of idealism. Those who whispered about his dubious character in those early days found themselves shut out and ignored.

Now we know for certain that Clinton was what we suspected all along. A liar and philanderer. But he is also a man who has abused his power, who has abused those who were weaker than him. Now that the lies of the Lewinsky affair have been exposed, do you really doubt that Paula Jones and Kathleen Willey (there are doubtless numerous others) were telling the truth? Remember Ms Jones, who said that the President had in fact exposed himself to her in an Arkansas hotel room. Or Ms Willey, who testified that the President had kissed and groped her against her will in the White House. Both women were in weak positions. Jones was a lowly clerk (later traduced by the Clinton spin machine as 'trailer trash') and Ms Willey was in need of a job. You may take the view that Clinton is telling the truth in denying his assaults on these women or you can, as I do, accept their version of events. Both have been smeared by the best dirty-tricks operation since Nixon's, both have had their reputations shredded in the public media.

The acts of consensual sex with a young intern are shabby but not the stuff that demand expulsion from political office. It is the abuse of clearly vulnerable women like Jones and Willey that make up the real stuff of impeachment. What makes the removal of Clinton instinctually difficult to countenance for liberals is the idea that it will represent a victory for the Republican right and all the ultra-conservative loonies who have long harboured a visceral hatred for the President. The snickering pleasure which the Lewinsky affair gives to Richard Nixon's heirs is one of the many depressing facets of this scandal. Newt Gingrich and his followers hated the promise of a just society which Clinton held out at the beginning of his first term; they helped to create a climate in which Americans grew to hate the idea of government and which led to the hobbling of Clinton's most ambitious plans to create healthcare and educational services worthy of a hugely wealthy country. Newt Gingrich and his corporate hyenas are not what America needs right now.

And yet it is to them that Mr Clinton, with his lies and recklessness and abuse, has handed the moral high ground. They have him where they want him, slowly roasting over a spit. They may well keep it up for the next two years, figuring with epic cynicism that a catastrophically damaged Clinton will ensure a Republican presidential victory. And so, like Clinton, they have made the pursuit of power for power's sake the defining ideal of American politics. There is a longer-term price to pay for this cynicism. I heard it in conversations on the streets of New York and Boston earlier this week. Repeatedly I was told that Clinton's sexual carry-on did not matter. The economy is doing fine, why worry? It is as if the events in Washington are a Hollywood movie, disconnected from the real lives and concerns of ordinary everyday America. This is understandable but tragic. Something bigger than Bill Clinton or Lewinsky or Gingrich is being dragged through the gutter. Democracy is being debased.

I suspect that Mr Clinton will hang on for as long as the Democratic Party allows him to do so. Only when the polls slip – and so far they are holding up just fine – will the grey men come and tell him it is time to go. They are a weak and divided bunch, mesmerized by the polls and slaves to their own ambitions. If Clinton did care about America, if he had a scintilla of concern for the contempt with which the next generation of Americans will view politics and government, he would resign now. By hanging on, Clinton is doing more than spoiling idealism. He is killing hope.

THE RAPE OF MICHAEL BLUCKER

New York, December 1998

Human rights groups in the United States launched a campaign against male rape, which, they say, is endemic in prisons across the country. An estimated three hundred thousand rapes are said to take place in American jails each year. But there are few prosecutions, the men are too ashamed, or too frightened, to report the offences.

Flying into La Guardia airport, the average out-of-towner will probably strain to see the Manhattan skyline through the aircraft's windows, but they may be rewarded with a view of the Long Island coastline or the borough of Queens. What they will almost certainly not notice – indeed I didn't until it was pointed out to me – is the low, flat island next to the airport. Rikers Island, New York City's main detention facility. A network of mini-prisons surrounded by acres of razor wire and beyond that, the waters of East River. Rikers: bleak, windswept and notorious. It is not a place you want to end up in.

I first heard of Rikers when reading an account of the death of the punk rocker Sid Vicious. He was sent there on remand after being accused of murdering his girlfriend. Once inside, Vicious was apparently set upon by fellow inmates, his nickname was a challenge. Vicious was repeatedly beaten and repeatedly raped. Nothing particularly strange about that in American prisons. Ask anybody, off the record, from cops to prison officers, most of all the prisoners themselves. It happens all the time. When you hear this mentioned casually on the outside, the import of the information doesn't quite sink in. RAPED. Men raping men. All the time. All over America. And then you step into the world of the prisons, you hear the testimony of the victims and the brute

194

reality hits you like a punch in the solar plexus. I hadn't been in Rikers long before I felt the atmosphere closing in. We were accompanied by guards, at no stage were we in any danger. But guards cannot stop stares, they cannot change the expression on men's faces, they cannot stop some of the toughest-looking men you have ever seen in your life wolf-whistling and leering. These days Rikers Island has one of the better reputations when it comes to prison rape. The authorities have cracked down on gangs in the prison and the number of violent incidents has been greatly reduced.

But after the stories I had been hearing over the previous few days, the wolf-whistles were making me very nervous. Stories like that of Ivory Rhodes, forced to share a cell with a black gang leader and raped at knifepoint. Ivory, who has been on the move from prison to prison ever since, to escape the stigma of being a rape victim. As Ivory and others explained it, a man who cannot resist a rapist is labelled a punk and becomes the sexual property of his attacker.

It was Michael Blucker, aged twenty-nine and married, who gave me the most graphic, let me say sickeningly graphic, portrait of the punk's life. Michael was serving time in an Illinois prison for burglary. His was not a violent crime. Yet Michael found himself locked up with some of the most violent men in the state and was the only white prisoner in a wing of more than a hundred and sixty men. Slender, with long brown hair and a boyish face, he was immediately singled out. It began with three gang members entering his cell, overpowering him and ripping off his clothes. One kept watch at the door, while one sodomized Michael and the third forced him to perform oral sex. The three men changed positions frequently. He did not fight back. He could not. Had he told the warders, he would have been killed, he said. Such is the prison's ruthless code of silence. Later, when he did complain, he says he was ignored, a common grievance of prison rape victims. The rapes kept happening. Once, in the shower, he was knocked out and gang-raped. 'I don't know if it was one, ten, fifteen or twenty of them,' he said. 'After a while I got tired of being beaten and I just went with the programme,' he explained. That meant submitting to a gang lord who, in return for protecting him from violent attack, forced Michael to sell his body to other inmates. The gangster naturally took the profits. So, in a typical day, he would be sodomized in one cell, perform oral sex in another, go to the prison yard and go through the same process with several other prisoners and then go to his room and wash. Any attempts to resist his 'owner's' orders and he was savagely beaten. When Michael talks about this his eyes seem to glaze over, he pauses and twitches. He talks about the guys who were 'nice' enough to use a condom, about the 'psycho' who beat him until he pretended to enjoy the rape.

And then he says that God has helped him come through this. That God has given him a new life. That God has healed him of the HIV virus he has contracted in prison. 'I believe,' he says. 'All you have to do is believe.'

THE NIGHT PINOCHET GOT MY NEIGHBOURS DRUNK

London, February 1999

The former Chilean dictator Augusto Pinochet was engaged in a legal battle in England. Spain wanted him extradited to face trial for crimes he was alleged to have committed while head of state. As the courts deliberated, there was also a public debate on how the elderly general should be treated.

My neighbour Alejandro and I share an interest in the poetry of Pablo Neruda. In the days when he lived in Chile's Isla Negra, Alejandro would see the old poet occasionally in the garden and wave to him. Neruda would wave back and in this way and through reading his work Alejandro came to feel he knew Neruda. This must have been in the early seventies, towards the end of Neruda's life when he had gone back to Chile after serving as Salvador Allende's ambassador to Paris. In those days Alejandro was an idealistic young leftist in a country sliding towards dramatic confrontation. He loved the *Canto General* (1950), filled with mystical evocations of the landscape and animals of Chile, and laments for the native world torn apart by Narvaes and others among the Conquistadores. The following lines from 'They Come for the Islands' are a rich example of Neruda's disavowal of the horrors inflicted by his Spanish forebears on Chile's Indians. In view of Chile's later history they seem especially chilling.

> The children of the clay saw their smiles smashed,
> battered their stance light as deer's,
> all the way to death they did not understand.
> They were trussed up and tortured,
> they were gnawed and buried.

197

And when time danced around again
waltzing among the palms
the green hall was empty.
Nothing was left but bones
rigidly fastened
in the form of a cross, to the greater
glory of God and of men.

One of the great regrets of Alejandro's life was that he did not attend Neruda's funeral, which took place just twelve days after Pinochet's coup. The burial became the focus of the first major demonstration against the new military regime. Soon after, rightists broke into Neruda's Santiago home and destroyed many books and papers. 'I have always regretted not going to the funeral . . . but the atmosphere was one of terror, pure terror and I was afraid to go,' he said.

Until we met for Christmas drinks at a friend's house the other night I did not really know Alejandro and his wife Paola. I knew they had come to London as exiles from Pinochet's Chile back in 1973. One daughter had returned to Chile after Pinochet gave way to a democratic government but the rest of the family still lives in Britain. They are quiet people and beyond the usual daily pleasantries we saw little of each other. In fact the discussion of Neruda at the drinks party was the first real conversation we'd had. Alejandro may have only watched Neruda from a distance but he was a close friend of Victor Jara, the songwriter, arrested and killed by Pinochet's forces after the coup. They had played in a band together. 'Pinochet and his people they feared art, they feared musicians and writers and that is why they wanted to stamp out people like Victor,' he said. Alejandro and Paola fled Chile four months after the coup as the net was closing in around the left-wingers and student activists still at large.

. Inevitably the subject of Pinochet's extended stay in Britain came up. Paola said she had been at the House of Lords on the day the appeal was allowed. The children, all of whom had been reared in Britain, went with her. They could not believe the decision and that night they went out and got drunk to celebrate. It was a Thursday night and there was work the following morning but the hangover was worth it. 'All of this thing has been a bit like a dream. None of it could have been expected,' she said. 'And if Pinochet is extradited to Spain it will be the best thing that has ever happened.' Alejandro, sitting next to her on the couch, nodded his head in agreement.

I have already written that I did not expect Pinochet to be extradited. That was before the Law Lords' judgment. I am still inclined to that view. So are Alejandro and Paola. What did I think would happen, they wanted to know. I said that Jack Straw is caught between a rock and a hard place. He is a member of a government that has loudly proclaimed its belief in human rights, his own political sensibilities suggest that he should take the side of the disappeared and tortured, and the highest law officers in the land say the old dictator should face his accusers in Spain. But there is a feeling, not just on the part of the right, that Chile's business is Chile's business, that how the country deals with its past really is a matter for the people of Chile. If their elected representatives agreed to give Pinochet and his cronies an amnesty, the argument goes, then what right has the British government to insist that they take another course? Alejandro said he knew all that. He had obviously been through these arguments countless times.

But even if there is no extradition they don't believe Pinochet should be simply packed on to a plane and sent home to Chile. There must at least be a moral sanction. So I have a suggestion. Agree to send him home but under the South Africa option: insist that in return for a one-way ticket to Santiago he apologizes to the families of the three thousand or so people who disappeared under his rule. Send a camera into the walled estate where he is resting, set it up in the sitting room and let General Pinochet do some talking. It is said that he is a proud old man who believes he saved his country from communism and economic ruin. True, Chile is now a prosperous place. But the price in dead and tortured is a price that should not and need not have been paid. And there has been no disclosure of the facts, not even a shred of remorse for the horrors of the coup years. Too many dictators – on the left and right – have gone to their graves without even the vaguest sanction. Think of the monster Mao, who sent millions to their deaths, or Stalin, the master of terror. They died in their beds, with no accusing fingers to trouble them. Pinochet is clearly not in the same league. But he shared with them an arrogant contempt for human rights.

Had Mao and Stalin also managed to deliver prosperity and stability to their people would we be told (as we are with Pinochet) that the sacrifice of human life and freedom before state power was justified? We have been down that road too often this century. Those who have suffered directly will feel such a compromise is dishonourable. But we must face some uncomfortable facts. Pinochet may well be dead by the time the case comes to trial in Spain. Even if he does make it to trial it is inconceivable that a Spanish court would send him to jail. I am reminded of a piece of writing by Primo Levi, who, having survived the Holocaust, was asked by another survivor whether he had been right to refuse forgiveness to a dying SS officer in one of the concentration camps. Levi wrote: 'Under these conditions, it is not always easy, indeed it is perhaps impossible, to assign an absolute value to right and wrong: it is in the nature of crime to create situations of moral conflict, dead ends of which bargaining and compromise are the only conditions of exit; conditions which inflict yet another wound on justice and on oneself.' Allowing Pinochet to go home will be a wound on justice. But if he talks before he goes, if he faces the world with a full statement of remorse for the suffering he caused, then something meaningful will have been achieved. From the mouth of Pinochet, at last, the truth.

INDEX

Adams, Gerry, 102, 104–5
Afghanistan, 172–5
Africa, renaissance in, 154–8
  see also individual African countries
Ahern, Chris, 23, 25
air strikes, 63, 64, 65, 66, 67, 69,
  72–4, 76–9, 83
Albania, 65–71
Albanian Serbs, expulsion of, 59–86
alcoholism, 3–11, 48–51
Alejandro, 197–200
Aleksander Palace Hotel, 66
All of Us (Carver), 51
Allende, Salvador, 197
America, partnership with Balkans,
  83–6
American jails, 194–6
ANC, 140
Angola, 159–61
anti-Americanism, 84
Arafat, Yasser, 178
Ardmore, Waterford, 24, 29
Ardoyne, Belfast, 111–16
Ards Peninsula, 4
Aris, Michael, 185–9
Arkan, 62
assignments overseas, 52–5
Associated Press television, 172
Atlantic bass, 29–30
Auden, W. H., 68
Aung San Suu Kyi, 185–9

B-Specials, 114
Baker, Father, 109
Balkans, 59–86
  United States partnership with, 83–6
Ballybunnion, 12, 15, 18
Ballylongford, 92
Ballymoney, killings at, 99, 105
Ballyquinn, 27, 29
Ballyseedy, 93
Ballysillan, 113
bass fishing, 27–30
BBC, 10
Beatles, 23
Beckett, Samuel, 9–10

Beijing, 168–71
Belfast, 3–4, 97, 111–16
Belgian troops, in Rwanda, 127
Bell, Martin, 52, 55
Bellow, Saul, 47
Benebikira sisters, 124, 126, 128–30
Black and Tans, 89, 92
Blair, Tony, 71, 76, 83
  ethnic cleansing and, 85
Blucker, Michael, rape of, 194–6
Bosnia-Herzegovina, 84
Bosnian war, 59
Boylan, Jimmy, 18–19
bribery, at road blocks, 54
Brink, Andre, 138
Britannia (royal yacht), 165
Brother Jerome (Jerome Kelly), 31–4
Buddhism, Aung San Suu Kyi and, 186
bullies, 39–41
Burma, 185–9
Butare, 119–35
Butare University Hospital, 123
Butugi, Mimoza, 66–7

Caliso, Waterford, 29
Camps Bay, South Africa, 144
Canto General (Neruda), 197
Cape Town, Christmas in, 144–7
Captain, Robert, 137
Carey, Peter, 44
Carter, Kevin, 137
Carver, Raymond, 27, 47–51
Catholic Church, 14, 31–4, 89
  Irishness and, 93
Chang, Joan, 172
Chianti, Tuscany, images in, 80–2
Chile, 197–200
China, 165–71
Chinese embassy, Belgrade, 72–3
Chinese food, 168–71
Christian brothers, 31
Claddagh ring, 52–3
Clark, Alan, 71
Clarke, Seamus, 112, 114, 115
Clashmelcon, 93
Clinton, Bill, 70, 76, 83, 190–3

Clounmacon, North Kerry, 17
Club Golbahar, 172–5
Cnoc on Oir (Mountain of Gold), 12
Collins, Michael, 89, 91, 105
colonialism, faults of, 155
Complete Works of William Shakespeare, The,
    10–11
Connaught Rangers, 107–10
Connolly, James, 109
Connor, Toddy, 18
Continental Hotel, Skopje, 64
Cork, 21–6, 177
    housing in, 33–4
Covent Garden, 10
crime, in Hong Kong, 167
Croatia, US support for, 84
Cumann Na Mban, 89
Curragh Strand, Waterford, 29
Cynthia (Mthebe), 139–43

Dai restuaurant, 168–71
Daly, Private James Joseph, 107–10
de Klerk, F. W., 98
De Valera, Eamon, 89
debating society, school, 32
decommissioning, in Northern Ireland,
    102
democracy, in Burma, 185–9
Deng Xiaoping, 169
dentists
    in Jerusalem, 176–8
    in Spain, 179–81
diarrhoea, 160, 174, 182–4
Dick, Father, 179–81
discrimination, Ulster and, 97
Donja Glumina, 61
Donnybrook, Dublin, 5
'Doodle, Thomas', 89–90
Dore, Tom, 115
Drumcree, 99–102
Dublin, 5, 37

Easter 1916 Rebellion, 92
'Easy' (chef from Mitrovica), 68–71,
    73, 83
education, 17
ethnic cleansing, 68–71, 84–6
    Drumcree and, 101

Falls Road, Belfast, 4
family farm, at Lisselton, 13

famine, in Ireland, 15
FAR (Forces Armée Rwandaise), 132
Faulkner, William, 47
Feale River, North Kerry, 18, 28
Fianna Fail, 89
Fine Gael, 89
fishing, 27–30
Fitzgerald, F. Scott, 47, 50, 165, 190
Ford, Henry, 19
Franschoek, South Africa, 147
Freetown, 151–3
fur trapping, 3–11

Gaelic football, 22, 111–16
Gallagher, Rory, 21, 22–3
Gallagher, Tess, 50
Garvaghy Road, 102
Genesis, 22
genocide, 76–9, 148–50
    in Rwanda, 119–35
    US and, 85
Gilvarry, Eamon, 113, 114, 116
Gilvarry, Maurice, 112, 113, 114,
    115–16
Gingrich, Newt, 192
Gjakova, men of, 70
Glencairn Avenue, Belfast, 3–4
Goat Island, 36
Golbahar, Afghanistan, 172–5
Good Friday Agreement, 96, 116
graves, mass, 61, 61–3
Great Gatsby, The (Fitzgerald), 50, 165,
    190
Great Railway Journeys, 44
'Grenade', 148–50
Grogan, Pat, 111, 112, 113, 115
Guinness, 13, 60
Gunn, Davy, 19
Gurtenard Wood, North Kerry, 18

Habyalimana, Jean, 124–5
Harrison, John, 137
Hassett, Michael, 35–8
Hategekimana, Lieutenant Ildephonse,
    129
Havel, Vaclav, 190
Hay-on-Wye, 43–6
Heaney, Seamus, 97, 177
'heart of darkness', 123, 154
Heathrow airport, 54, 64, 144
Hemingway, Ernest, 47

INDEX

Hitler, Adolf, 76–9
HIV, 196
Holocaust, 77–9
Holy Cross, football team, 111–16
home, leaving, 52–5
Hong Kong, 165–7
horse sashimi, 182–4
Hotel Ibis, 119–20, 123
house-building programme, in Cork, 33–4
Hout Bay, South Africa, 145
Hudson Bay Trading Company, 4–5, 8, 10–11
Human Rights Watch, 131
'Hummingbird' (Carver), 50
Humphrys, John, 44
Hutus, 120–35

idealism, spoiled, 190–3
insect bites, 172–5
International War Crimes Tribunal, 134
interviewing, questioning of, 148–50
Ireland, Northern, 96–107, 111–16, 155–6, 177
Irish, as Catholic, 93
Irish language, 90
Irish Republican Army (IRA), 16, 91, 98, 104
    at Soloheadbeg, 108
    ethnic cleansing and, 101
Israel, dentists in, 176–8
Israelis, US support for, 84
Iwata, Mrs, 183–4
Izetbegovic, 60

Jacob, Dr, 177–8
jails, male rape in, 194–6
Japan, 182–4
Jara, Victor, 198
Jerusalem, toothache in, 176–8
Johannesburg, 26, 136–8
Jones, David, 100
Jones, Paula, 191–2
Jonno (cameraman), 172–5
Jullundur, Amritsar, 108–9

Kabbah, President Ahmed Tejan, 151
Kabila, Laurent, 156–7
Kabul, Afghanistan, 174
Kajuga, Robert, 120
Kanyabugoyi, Emery, 126–30

Kanyabugoyi, Mrs Speciose, 126–8, 135
Kanyabugoyi, Thierry, 126–30
Karenzi, Professor Pierre, 125–6, 127
Karenzi, Solange, 128
Kasrils, Ronnie, 26
Keane, Bill (grandfather), 17
Keane, Conor (cousin), 16, 19
Keane, Daniel (son), 43, 45–6, 53
    bullying and, 39–41
    fishing and, 30
Keane, Eamonn (brother), 23, 25
Keane, Eamonn Patrick (father), 3–11, 14, 48–9
Keane, Hannie, née Purtill (grandmother), 12, 16, 91
Keane, John B. (uncle), 6, 7, 14–15, 18–20, 89–90, 94
Kelly, Jerome (Brother Jerome), 31–4
Kenneally, Professor Brendan, 92–3
Kennedy, Robert, 112
Kenya, 157
Kerry, 7, 12–20
    fishing and, 27–30
Kiernan, Michael, 32
Kigali, Rwanda, 126, 127, 148–50
King, Martin Luther, 112
Kinyarwanda, in South London, 132
Knockanure, 92
Kosovo, 63, 64–7, 68, 72–5, 76–9, 83–6
    images in Tuscany, 80–2
    seen in Rwanda, 121
Krajina Serbs, 84
Kukes, Albania, 69, 72–5
Kyushu, Japan, 182–4

L'Amola, Tuscany, 81
land, passion for, 14–15
'Late Fragment' (Carver), 51
leaving home, 52–5
Levi, Primo, 200
Lewinsky, Monica, 190–3
Libdeh, Dr Abu, 177
Lisselton, North Kerry, 12, 13
Listowel, North Kerry, 12, 18–19
literary festivals, 43–6
Little, Allan, 136, 138
London, Eamonn Patrick Keane in, 8–10
Long Kesh, prison at, 115

INDEX

Luanda, 159–60
Lucknow, prison at, 110

McAleese, Mary, 107
Macedonia, refugees and, 64–7
McGuinness, Martin, 102, 104–5
MacNeice, Louis, 10, 98
male rape, in US jails, 194–6
Malley, Eric, 28–9
Mandela, Nelson, 98, 136, 139, 140,
        144, 187
Manhattan, 194
Mao Tse-tung, 200
Marcus, Dr, 160
Masood Ahmed Shah, 172
mass graves, 61–3
massage, 184
Mathom, Victor, 140
media, faults of, 155–6
mercenaries, 153
Messines Ridge, 107
Michael, in Rwanda, 121–2, 135
Mills, Ian, 26
Milosevic, Slobodan, 60, 66, 70–1,
        83, 86
    judging of, 76–9
Mobutu, 156
Moi, Daniel arap, 154, 157
Montenegro, 86
Moreland, Martin, 188
Mthebes, Cynthia, 139–43
Mukarabayiza, Sister Speciose, 123–4,
        129–30
Murphy, Ciaran, 112, 113, 114, 115
Murphy, Pat, 112, 113, 114, 115, 116
Muvunyi, Lt Colonel Tharcisse, 125,
        129–34

NATO bombing, 63, 65, 66, 67, 69,
        72–4, 76–9, 83
NATO expansionism, 84
Neruda, Pablo, 197–8
Netanyahu, Binyamin, 178
New Path to the Waterfall, A (Carver), 50
New York, 35–8, 194–6
Newport station, 43–4
Nigeria, 157
Nin, Chinese actor, 168–71
Nixon, Richard, 191, 192
Nkosi, Milton, 137
Noordhoek, South Africa, 145

North Kerry, 7, 12–20, 27–30
Northern Ireland, 96–107, 111–16,
        155–6, 177
Nsabimana, Sylvain, 125, 131
Nyshamuriya, Jean Birchmans, 125

'Old Days, The' (Carver), 49
Omagh, bomb at, 103–6
Orangemen, 99–102
Osmanovic, Rifat, 63
overseas assignments, 52–5

Paisley, Ian, 100
Palestinians, 176–8
Panorama, 140
Paola, 198–200
Parnell, Charles Stewart, 90
partition, of Ireland, 89, 91, 92–3
passions, in North Kerry, 14
Patten, Chris, 165
Patten, Joel, 100–2
peace process, Ireland and, 96
Pearse Patrick, 93
People's Liberation Army, 169
Peres, Shimon, 178
'Photograph of My Father in His
        Twenty-second Year' (Carver), 48
Piercy, Paul, 8–11
Pink Floyd, 22
Pinochet, Augusto, 197–200
Placide ('Grenade'), 148–50
Pogradec, 67
Prague Spring, 112
Presentation Brothers, 31–4
Presidential Guard, Rwanda, 125
Prince, Tony, 22
Protestants, in Ulster, 97–102
Purtill, Hannie see Keane, Hannie
Purtill, Madge, 13
Purtill, Mick, 89
Purtill, Willie, 12, 13
Purtill family, 12–14

Quinn brothers, killing of, 99–102, 105

Radio Caroline, 22
Radio Luxembourg, 22
railways, 43–4
Rangoon, 187
rape, in US jails, 194–6
Real IRA, 104

INDEX

refugees
  Albania and, 68–75
  in Macedonia, 64–7
religious fanatics, 46
Rhodes, Ivory, 195
Rikers Island, New York, 194–5
Riyalda, 59–61
road blocks, 54
Robben Island, 144
rock 'n' roll, 21–6
Rolling Stones, 23
Royal Irish Constabulary (RIC), 16, 92
Royal Ulster Constabulary (RUC), 114
Rwanda, 60, 77, 119–35
  questioning in, 148–50
  US and, 85
Ryan, John, 28–30

St Declans, Ardmore, 24
salmon, 28
Santander, 179–81
Santiago de Compostela, 179–81
Sarajevo, 59–63
sashimi, horse, 182–4
Scarborough, South Africa, 145
Scott, Fred, 172
sea angling, 29–30
'Second Coming, The' (Yeats), 103
Shankill Road, Belfast, 4
Share, in Cork, 33–4
Sheriff, Abdul, 137
Shipster, Michael, 26
Simonstown, South Africa, 146
Sinn Fein, 98, 102
Skelly, Joe, 111, 112, 114
Skopje, 64–7
Snipers Alley, 59
socialism, in China, 169
Soloheadbeg, County Tipperary, 108
South Africa, 25–6, 98, 136–8, 144–7
South, David 'Tubby', 183–4
Soyinka, Wole, 156
Spain, toothache in, 179–81
Spirit of Drumcree group, 100–102
Spring Street, New York, 35, 38
Stabrook, Keno, 137
Stalin, Joseph, 76, 78, 200
Stefan, Dr, 61–2
story-telling, 16
Straw, Jack, 199

Table Mountain, 144, 145
teaching, 31–4
Tembisa, South Africa, 139–43
'Ten Songs' (Auden), 68
Terre'Blanche, Eugene, 136
'They Come For the Islands' (Neruda), 197–8
Thompson, Hunter S., 46
Thornton, Father, 145
'Toad Kings', 156
Today, 44
toothache
  in Israel, 176–8
  in Spain, 179–81
Tralee, 18
Treaty, in Ireland, 91
Trimble, David, 100, 102
Troubles, in Ireland, 94, 96–106, 111–16
Truth and Reconciliation Commission, 138
Tudjman, 60, 84, 86
turtle soup, 170–1
Tuscany, 80–2
Tutsis, 78, 120–35
Tuzla, 61

Uganda, 157
Uige, 160–1
Ulster, 96
Ulster Protestants, 97–102
Ulster Volunteer Force (UVF), 115
Unionism, 100–102
United States
  in partnership with Balkans, 83–6
  spoiled idealism and, 190–3

Vergemount Hospital, Dublin, 6
Vicious, Sid, 194
Villa Vignamaggio, Tuscany, 80–2

Watergate, 191
Whiting Bay, Waterford, 29
Willey, Kathleen, 191–2
Wilson, Nicky, 6
Witsands, South Africa, 145
World Food Programme, 72

Yeats, W. B., 70, 95, 103
Yes (group), 22

Zvornik, 61–2